VINEGAR

1001 Practical Household Uses

Contents

Originally published in 2007 by L&K Designs. This edition published in 2010 by Myriad Books Limited.

© L&K Designs 2007
PRINTED IN CHINA

Publishers Disclaimer

The uses, hints, tips and ideas contained in this book are passed on in good faith but the publisher cannot be held responsible for any adverse results.

The History of Vinegar

The accidental discovery in ancient times that grape juice, left undisturbed, turns into wine was a cause for celebration. Wine has been used in celebrations ever since. The subsequent and inevitable discovery that wine, left undisturbed, eventually turns into vinegar was not heralded with as much enthusiasm. However, over many long years the wonders of vinegar have been revealed, and will continue to be for many years to come.

Ancients very quickly uncovered the tremendous versatility of vinegar. While records were not kept before 5000 BC legend has it that the Sumerians, a civilization of ancient Babylonia, used vinegar as a cleaning agent. The Babylonians discovered that vinegar slows or stops the action of bacteria that spoils food so they used it as a preservative. They also used it as a condiment.

Caesar's armies used vinegar as a beverage. The Egyptian queen, Cleopatra, demonstrated its solvency powers by dissolving precious pearls in vinegar to win a wager that she could consume a fortune in a single meal. Helen of Troy apparently bathed in vinegar to relax. Hannibal, the famous African General, used vinegar to help his army cross the Alps. According to the writings of Titus Livius, a historian who lived around the time of Christ, obstructive boulders were heated and drenched in vinegar. This action cracked the boulders into small pieces, allowing them to be easily moved away.

Vinegar has been revered throughout the ages. There are many Biblical references in both the Old and New Testaments that reveal the use of vinegar as a beverage, likely diluted and sweetened. In fact, the scriptures say that Jesus drank vinegar just before he was crucified. There are also Biblical references to the use of vinegar as a condiment to dip bread and as a remedy for infections and wounds. Vinegar is also mentioned in the Talmud where it is called for to make haroseth in Pesachim. Vinegar became one of our first medicines around 400 BC. Hippocrates, a Greek physician and writer, known as the father of medicine, extolled vinegar's therapeutic qualities. He prescribed drinking vinegar to his patients for many ailments.

Vinegar came to the rescue in the Middle Ages in some extraordinary ways. During the Black Plague in Europe, thieves poured vinegar over their skin to protect themselves from germs before robbing the dead. During the seventeenth century in Europe and England vinegar was used as a deodorizer. Citizens held sponges soaked in vinegar to their noses to reduce the smell of raw sewage in the streets. Women conveniently carried vinegar-laden sponges in small silver boxes and men stored them in their walking canes. The powerful British Navy used vinegar to preserve food during long sea voyages and to clean the decks of their ships.

In modern times vinegar continues to play a valuable role in society. During World War I vinegar was used to treat wounds on the battlefields. Today, white vinegar is recommended for the treatment of rashes, bites and other minor ailments when camping.

Vinegar has become most popular, however, as a condiment on chips and as an ingredient in food and baking. The virtues of speciality vinegars, such as balsamic and rice vinegars areproclaimed with increasing passion by food connoisseurs. Vinegar is still used for pickling and preserving, but less so, as people have less time for this fine craft.

For centuries women have used white vinegar for cleaning and have passed on their usage tips through their family. However, in our time-pressed world many of the great and varied uses for vinegar have been forgotten. This book provides a broad range of vinegar usage tips that are convenient to use and that really work.

It is hoped that history is in the making and that vinegar will become increasingly popular as an all-purpose household cleaner. The advantages to the purse, the planet and our health, compared to toxic cleaners, will hopefully speak for themselves.

The Production of Vinegar

Vinegar is made from the oxidation of ethanol in wine, cider, beer, fermented fruit juice, or nearly any other liquid containing alcohol. Commercial vinegar is produced either by fast or slow fermentation processes. Slow methods are generally used with traditional vinegars and fermentation proceeds slowly over the course of weeks or months. The longer fermentation period allows for the accumulation of a nontoxic slime composed of acetic acid bacteria and soluble cellulose, known as the mother of vinegar.

Fast methods add mother of vinegar (i.e bacterial culture) to the source liquid and then add air using a venturi pump system or a turbine to promote oxygenisation to give the fastest fermentation. In fast production processes, vinegar may be produced in a period ranging between 20 hours and three days. Vinegar eels (Turbatrix aceti), a form of nematode, may occur in some forms of vinegar. These feed on the mother and occur in naturally fermenting vinegar . Most manufacturers filter and pasteurize their product before bottling to prevent these organisms from forming.

Types of Vinegar
White

So-called "white vinegar" (actually transparent in appearance) can be made by oxidizing a distilled alcohol. Alternatively, it may be nothing more than a solution of acetic acid in water. Most commercial white vinegars are 5 acetic acid solutions. They are made from grain (often maize) and water. White vinegar is used for culinary as well as cleaning purposes.

Malt

Malt vinegar is made by malting barley, causing the starch in the grain to turn to maltose. An ale is then brewed from the maltose and allowed to turn into vinegar, which is then aged. It is typically light brown in colour. A cheaper alternative, called "non-brewed condiment," is a solution of 4-8 acetic acid coloured with caramel. There is also around 1-3 citric acid present. Non-brewed condiment is more popular in the North of England, and gained popularity with the rise of the Temperance Societies. The non-alcoholic nature of non-brewed condiment therefore makes it popular for individuals whose cultural or religious beliefs forbid them from drinking alcohol.

Wine

Wine vinegar is made from red or white wine, and is the most commonly used vinegar in Mediterranean countries and Germany. As with wine, there is a considerable range in quality. Better quality wine vinegars are matured in wood for up to two years and exhibit a complex, mellow flavour. There are more expensive wine vinegars made from individual varieties of wine, such as champagne or sherry.

Apple cider

Apple cider vinegar, sometimes known simply as cider vinegar, is made from cider or apple must, and is often sold unfiltered, with a brownish-yellow colour; it often contains mother of vinegar. It is currently very popular, partly due to its beneficial health and beauty properties.

Fruit

Fruit vinegars are made from fruit wines without any additional flavouring. Common flavours of fruit vinegar include blackcurrant, raspberry, quince, and tomato. Typically, the flavours of the original fruits remain tasteable in the final vinegar. Most such vinegars are produced in Europe, where there is a growing market for high priced vinegars made solely from specific fruits (as opposed to non-fruit vinegars which are infused with fruits or fruit flavours). Persimmon vinegar is popular in South Korea, and jujube vinegar is produced in China. Umeboshi vinegar, a salty, sour liquid that is a by-product of umeboshi (pickled ume) production, is produced in Japan but is technically not a true vinegar.

Balsamic

Balsamic vinegar is an aromatic, aged type of vinegar traditionally manufactured in Modena, Italy, from the concentrated juice, or must, of white grapes (typically of the Trebbiano variety). It is very dark brown in colour and its flavour is rich, sweet, and complex, with the finest grades being the end product of years of aging in a successive number of casks made of various types of wood (including oak, mulberry, chestnut, cherry, juniper, ash, and acacia). Originally an artisanal product available only to the Italian upper classes, balsamic vinegar became widely known and available around the world in the late 20th century. True balsamic is aged between 3 and 12 years and is expensive. The commercial balsamic sold in supermarkets is typically made with red wine vinegar or concentrated grape juice mixed with a strong vinegar which is laced with caramel and sugar. However produced, balsamic needs to be made from a grape product. Balsamic has a high acid level, but the sweetness covers the tart flavour, making it very mellow.

Rice

Rice vinegar is most popular in the cuisines of East and Southeast Asia. It is available in white (actually light yellow), red, and black variants. The Japanese prefer a light and more delicate rice vinegar for the preparation of sushi rice. Red rice vinegar is traditionally coloured with red yeast rice, although some Chinese brands use artificial food colouring instead. Black rice vinegar is most popular in China, although it is also produced in Japan (see East Asian black). It may be used as a substitute for balsamic vinegar, although its dark colour and the fact that it is aged may be the only similarity between the two products. Some varieties of rice vinegar are sweetened or otherwise seasoned with spices or other added flavourings.

Coconut

Coconut vinegar, made from the sap, or "toddy," of the coconut palm, is used extensively in Southeast Asian cuisine (particularly in the Philippines, a major producer of the product), as well as in some cuisines of India. A cloudy white liquid, it has a particularly sharp, acidic taste with a slightly yeasty note.

Cane

Cane vinegar, made from sugar cane juice, is most popular in the Ilocos Region of the northern Philippines (where it is called sukang iloko), although it is also produced in France and the United States. It ranges from dark yellow to golden brown in colour and has a mellow flavour, similar in some respects to rice vinegar, though with a somewhat "fresher" taste. Contrary to expectation, it is not sweeter than other vinegars, containing no residual sugar.

Raisin

Vinegar made from raisins is used in cuisines of the Middle East, and is produced in Turkey. It is cloudy and medium brown in colour, with a mild flavour.

Date

Vinegar made from dates is a traditional product of the Middle East.

Beer

Vinegar made from beer is produced in Germany, Austria, and the Netherlands. Although its flavour depends on the particular type of beer from which it is made, it is often described as having a malty taste. That produced in Bavaria is a light golden colour, with a very sharp and not overly complex flavour.

Honey

Vinegar made from honey is rare, though commercially available honey vinegars are produced in Italy and France.

East Asian black

Chinese black vinegar is an aged product made from rice, wheat, millet, or sorghum, or a combination thereof. It has an inky black colour and a complex, malty flavour. There is no fixed recipe and thus some Chinese black vinegars may contain added sugar, spices, or caramel colour. The most popular variety, Chinkiang vinegar, originated in the city of Zhenjiang, in the eastern coastal province of Jiangsu, China, and is also produced in Tianjin and Hong Kong. A somewhat lighter form of black vinegar, made from rice, is also produced in Japan, where it is called kurozu. Since 2004 it has been marketed as a healthful drink; its manufacturers claim that it contains high concentrations of amino acids.

Flavoured vinegars

Popular fruit-flavoured vinegars include those infused with whole raspberries, blueberries, or figs (or else from flavourings derived from these fruits). Some of the more exotic fruit-flavoured vinegars include blood orange and pear. Herb vinegars are flavoured with herbs, most commonly Mediterranean herbs such as thyme or oregano. Such vinegars can be prepared at home by adding sprigs of fresh or dried herbs to vinegar bought from shops; generally a light-coloured, mild tasting vinegar such as that made from white wine is used for this purpose. Sweetened vinegar is of Cantonese origin and is made from rice wine, sugar and herbs including ginger, cloves and other spices.

Laundry

For all hints and tips in the laundry section, use white distilled vinegar.

Do not use vinegar if you add bleach to your rinse water as it will produce harmful vapours.

Clean your washing machine

An easy way to periodically clean out soap scum and disinfect your washing machine washer is to pour in 450ml (2 cups) of white distilled vinegar, then run the machine through a full cycle without any clothes or detergent.

Fabric conditioning

Instead of expensive fabric conditioners, add 275ml (1/2 pint) of white distilled vinegar to your rinse cycle which will keep your linens soft.

Preventative Measures

Anti-bacterial rinse

If you add 275ml (1/2 pint) of white distilled vinegar to your rinse cycle this will kill any remaining bacteria.

Colour Fading

To brighten your colours, instead of using that costly all-colour bleach, you can get the same results using vinegar. Just add 275ml (1/2 pint) white distilled vinegar to your machine's wash cycle to brighten up the colours in each load.

Colour Running

If you buy a piece of clothing or fabric that you think will run, soak your new garments in a few cups of undiluted white distilled vinegar for 10-15 minutes before their first washing. You can also add 225ml (1 cup) of white distilled vinegar to the last rinse, and that will set the colour of your newly dyed fabrics.

Lint reduction

Add 275ml (1/2 pint) of white distilled vinegar to your rinse cycle and you will notice a dramatic reduction in lint on your clothes.

Preventative Measures (continued)

Make new clothes ready to wear

Get the chemicals, dust, odour, and whatever else out of your brand-new or secondhand clothes by pouring 225ml (1 cup) of white distilled vinegar into the wash cycle the first time you wash them which will increase the life of the garment.

Soap residue

Eliminate soap residue by adding 275ml (1/2 pint) of white distilled vinegar to your rinse cycle.

Static cling

Reduce static cling in clothes by adding 275ml (1/2 pint) of white distilled vinegar to your rinse cycle.

Swimming Costumes

White distilled vinegar is also great for preserving the colour of swimming costumes. Put a little in water and soak your new swimwear, and the colour will last a lot longer even if you swim a lot in pools with lots of chlorine.

Tights

When washing nylon tights, adding white distilled vinegar to the water will prolong their lifespan.

Remedies

Blankets

Wool and cotton blankets come out soft and fluffy if you add 500ml (approx. 3/4 pint) white distilled vinegar to your rinse cycle.

Get the yellow out of clothing

To restore yellowed clothing, let the garments soak overnight in a solution of 12 parts warm water to 1 part white distilled vinegar. Wash them the following morning.

Shrunken woollens

Shrunken woollen jumpers and other items can usually be stretched back to their original size or shape after washing them in a solution of 1 part white wine vinegar to 2 parts water for 25 minutes. Let the garment air-dry after you've finished stretching it.

Whiten Sports Socks

Add 225ml (1 cup) white distilled vinegar to 1.5 litres (approx. 2 1/2 pints) tap water in a large pot. Bring the solution to a boil, then pour it into a bucket and drop in your dingy socks. Let them soak overnight then next day, wash them as you normally would.

Odour Removal

When the weather is hot and when a load of laundry doesn't get dried soon enough or fast enough – it gets that musty mildew smell - re-wash the clothes adding 275 ml (1/2 pint) of white distilled vinegar in the rinse cycle.

Cigarette smells on clothes

To get the lingering smell of cigarette smoke out of your good suit or dress, you can remove the smell without having to take your clothes to the dry cleaner. Just add 275 ml (1/2 pint) of white distilled vinegar to a bathtub filled with the hottest water from your tap. Close the door and hang your garments above the steam. The smell should be gone after a few hours.

Deodorising Wool jumpers

Handwash in luke warm water then rinse in equal parts of white distilled vinegar and water to remove lingering odours.

Diesel Spills

If diesel is spilled on clothes, the smell is horrible and refuses to go away. A little vinegar added to the washer takes most (if not all) the smell out.

Remove bleach odours

If using bleach for stain removal, add 275 ml (1/2 pint) vinegar to the final rinse to remove the bleach smell.

Stain Removal

Stain Removal - Bloodstains

It is important to treat the stains on your clothing as soon as possible as bloodstains are relatively easy to remove before they dry but can be nearly impossible to wash out after 24 hours. If you can get to the stain before it sets, treat it by pouring full-strength white distilled vinegar on the spot. Let it soak in for 5-10 minutes, then blot well with a cloth or towel. Repeat if necessary, then wash immediately.

Stain Removal - Crayon stains

Kids often manage to get crayon marks on their clothing. You can easily get these stains off by rubbing them with a recycled toothbrush soaked in undiluted white distilled vinegar before washing them.

Stain Removal - Deodorant

You can also remove deodorant stains from your washable shirts and blouses by gently rubbing the spot with undiluted white distilled vinegar before laundering. Wash as usual in the hottest water that's safe for the fabric.

Stain Removal - Dried-in stains

Older, dried-in stains will often come out in the wash after being pretreated with a solution of 3 tablespoons white distilled vinegar and 2 tablespoons liquid detergent in 1 litre warm water. Rub the solution into the stain, then blot it dry before washing.

Stain Removal - Ink

Treat the stain by first wetting it with some white distilled vinegar, then rub in a paste of 2 parts vinegar to 3 parts cornflour. Allow the paste to thoroughly dry before washing the item.

Stain Removal - Pretreat perspiration stains

Pour a bit of white distilled vinegar directly onto the stain, and rub it into the fabric before placing the item in the wash.

Stain Removal - Remove rings from collars and cuffs

Scrub the stained area of the material with a paste made from 2 parts white distilled vinegar to 3 parts baking soda. Let the paste set for half an hour before washing. This approach also works to remove light mildew stains from clothing.

Stain Removal - Rust Stains

To remove a rust stain from your cotton work clothes, moisten the spot with some full-strength white distilled vinegar and then rub in a bit of salt. If it's warm outdoors, let it dry in the sunlight (otherwise a sunny window will do), then wash as normal.

Stain Removal - Sponge out serious stains

Cola, hair dye, ketchup, and wine stains on washable cotton blends should be treated as soon as possible (that is, within 24 hours). Sponge the area with undiluted white distilled vinegar and wash immediately afterward. For really bad stains, add 250ml to 500ml (up to a pint) of vinegar to the wash cycle as well.

Stain Removal - Water-soluble stains

You can lift out many water-soluble stains - including beer, orange and other fruit juices, black coffee or tea, and vomit - from your cotton-blend clothing by patting the spot with a cloth or towel moistened with undiluted white distilled vinegar just before placing it in the wash. For large stains, you may want to soak the garment overnight in a solution of 3 parts white distilled vinegar to 1 part cold water before washing.

Suede stains

To eliminate a fresh grease spot on a suede jacket or skirt, gently brush it with a soft toothbrush dipped in white distilled vinegar. Let the spot air-dry, then brush with a suede brush. Repeat if necessary. You can also generally tone up suede items by lightly wiping them with a sponge dipped in white distilled vinegar.

Ironing

Cleaning your Iron - Inside

To eliminate mineral deposits and prevent corrosion on your steam iron, give it an occasional cleaning by filling the reservoir with undiluted white distilled vinegar.

Place the iron in an upright position, switch on the steam setting, and let the vinegar steam through it for 5-10 minutes. Then refill the chamber with clean water and repeat. Finally, give the water chamber a good rinsing with cold, clean water.

Cleaning your Iron - Cleaning the soleplate

To remove scorch marks from the soleplate of your iron, scrub it with a paste made by heating up equal parts white distilled vinegar and salt in a small pan. Use a rag dipped in clean water to wipe away the remaining residue.

Getting rid of old Hemlines

Moisten the area with a cloth dipped in equal parts white distilled vinegar and water, then place it under the garment before you start ironing.

Scorch marks

Eliminate slight scorch marks by rubbing the spot with a cloth dampened with white distilled vinegar, then blotting it with a clean towel.

Sharp creases

You'll find the creases in your freshly ironed clothes coming out a lot neater if you lightly spray them with equal parts water and white distilled vinegar before ironing them. For extra sharp creases in trouser and shirts, first dampen the garment using a cloth moistened in a solution of 1 part white distilled vinegar and 2 parts water. Then place a brown paper bag over the crease and start ironing.

Shiny seat marks

Brush the area lightly with a soft recycled toothbrush dipped in equal parts white distilled vinegar and water, then pat dry with a soft towel.

Wrinkle removal

Remove wrinkles out of clothes after drying by misting them with a solution of 1 part white distilled vinegar to 3 parts water. Spray the entire surface area thoroughly, hang it up and let it air-dry. You may find this approach works better for some clothes than ironing; it's certainly a lot gentler on the material.

Baby Care/Skin Care

Baby Clothes

For babies with sensitive skin use half the recommended detergent during the wash and skip the fabric softener. Instead, put the clothes through an additional rinse at the end and fill the softener dispenser with white distilled vinegar. This both sterilizes and neutralizes any residue left by the detergent which may cause your baby's sensitive skin to react.

Sensitive Skin

If you suffer from sensitive skin, follow the advice above for baby clothes and this could help prevent outbreaks and irritations.

Terry Nappies

Dilute 275 ml (1/2 pint) white distilled vinegar in 9 litres (approx 16 pints) of water and place in a nappy pail or bucket to neutralise the urine and help prevent staining. Soak and wash as usual.

Terry Nappies - Prevent skin irritation

Add 275ml (1/2 pint) white distilled vinegar during the rinse cycle to equalise the PH balance and help prevent skin irritation and nappy rash.

Shoes

Patent Leather

Bring an extra shine to patent leather by wiping shoes over with a soft cloth moistened with white distilled vinegar.

Sticker Removal

Remove price stickers from the sole of shoes by soaking a cloth in undiluted white distilled vinegar and then covering the sticker for several minutes until the liquid penetrates the sticker. Once soaked, the sticker should remove easily without leaving any residue.

Water marks on leather

Using 1 tablespoon of white distilled vinegar to 275ml (1/2 pint) of water, dampen a cloth and wipe away salt and water residue.

All-purpose cleaners

1) Fill a recycled spray bottle with 2 parts water, 1 part distilled white vinegar, and a couple of drops of washing-up liquid. This will make an effective quick-clean solution.

Suitable for glass, stainless steel, and plastic laminate surfaces.

2) Fill a recycled spray bottle with a cleaning solution made from 110ml (1/2 cup) white distilled vinegar, 225ml (1 cup) ammonia and 1/4 cup baking soda in 3.7 litres (1 gallon) water. Spritz it on spots and stains whenever needed and wipe off with a clean towel.

Suitable for cleaning walls and other painted surfaces.

3) To make an effective scouring mix which can be safely used on all of your metal cookware, including copper pots and pans, combine equal parts salt and flour and add just enough white distilled vinegar to make a paste. Work the paste around the cooking surface and the outside of the utensil, then rinse off with warm water and dry thoroughly with a soft dish towel.

Suitable for cleaning pots and pans.

Pesticide

Countertops and plastic surfaces
Mix equal parts white distilled vinegar and water and wipe over surface. In addition to cleaning the surface, the solution acts as an insect repellant.

Cupboards
Fill a small bowl with 375ml (approx. 1-1/2 cups) of apple cider vinegar and add a couple of drops of washing-up liquid. Leave it in there for a week; it will attract the bugs, which will fall into the bowl and drown.

Fly trap
Make a trap for flies by filling an old jar about halfway with apple cider vinegar. Punch a few holes in the lid, screw the lid back on and the flies will crawl through the holes.

Kitchen and utility room

Aluminium cookware

To remove dark stains (caused by cooking acidic foods) mix 1 teaspoon of white distilled vinegar for every cup of water needed to cover the stains. Let it boil for a couple of minutes, then rinse with cold water.

Aluminium utensils

Bring back the shine by boiling in a solution of 2 tablespoons of white distilled vinegar in 1 3/4 pints (1 litre) of water.

Breadbox

Clean and disinfect by wiping with full strength white distilled vinegar. Also helps eliminate odours.

Bottles and decanters

Place a dessertspoon of salt in a bottle or decanter and moisten with white distilled vinegar. Shake vigorously and then rinse with cold water.

Ceramic Tiles - Floor

Add between 250 to 500ml (up to a pint) of white distilled vinegar to a bucket of water to mop ceramic floor tiles. This is quicker than mopping with detergent as no rinsing is needed.

Ceramic Tiles - Wall

Mix a solution of 1 part white distilled vinegar to 3 parts water and use a cloth to wipe tiles clean. This also preserves the colour of the grout.

China

Remove tea, coffee and other lingering stains from china by submerging in a cleaning solution made from boiling equal parts of white distilled vinegar and water. Soak for an hour and then rinse with clean water before use. For stubborn stains, try scrubbing with equal parts white distilled vinegar and salt. Rinse with warm clean water.

Cloths & Sponges

Keep cloths and sponges smelling fresh by soaking overnight in a solution of 55ml (1/4 cup) of white distilled vinegar and water. Rinse thoroughly before use.

Chrome

Apply a light misting of undiluted white vinegar from a recycled spray bottle. Buff with a soft cloth to bring out the brightness.

Coffeemaker

Fill the decanter with 450ml (2 cups) white distilled vinegar and 225ml (1 cup) water. Place a filter in the machine, and pour the solution into the coffeemaker's water chamber. Turn on the coffeemaker and let it run through a full brew cycle. Remove the filter and replace it with a fresh one. Then run clean water through the machine for two full cycles, replacing the filter again for the second brew.

Containers/Storage jars

Clean and disinfect by wiping with full strength white distilled vinegar.

Cutting Boards

Clean and disinfect by wiping with full strength white distilled vinegar.

Dishwasher

General Cleaning

Remove built-up soap film and increase performance by pouring 225ml (1 cup) undiluted white distilled vinegar into the bottom of the unit, or in a bowl on the top rack. Then run the machine through a full cycle without any dishes or detergent.

Note: If there is no mention of vinegar in your dishwasher owner's manual, check with the manufacturer first.

Dishwasher - Glassware, Everyday

Add 55ml (1/4 cup) white distilled vinegar in the rinse aid dispenser of the dishwasher to eliminate spots and cloudiness.

Dishwasher - Glassware, Crystal and Fine Cut Glass

Add 2 tablespoons of white distilled vinegar to dishwasher, then rinse in a solution of 3 parts warm water to 1 part white distilled vinegar and allow to air-dry.

Drains - Deodorize

Using a funnel, pour 115g (1/2 cup) of baking soda followed by 225ml (1 cup) of white distilled vinegar down the drain. When the foaming subsides, flush with hot tap water. Wait five minutes, and then flush again with cold water. This will kill odour-causing bacteria.

Drains - Improve drain speed

To speed up a slow drain, pour in 115g (1/2 cup) of salt followed by 450ml (2 cups) of boiling white distilled vinegar. Flush through with hot and cold tap water.

Drains - Unblock

Following the methods above for deodorizing and improving drainage should also remove any blockage.

Egg Poacher

Prevent discolouration on egg poachers by adding 1 teaspoon of white distilled vinegar to the water when poaching eggs.

Fryer

Clean fat fryers after use by boiling out fat with an equal solution of water and white distilled vinegar. This is cost effective and safe, with no chemicals or risk of fire.

Frying Pan/Skillet

Boiling 450ml (2 cups) white distilled vinegar in your frying pan for 10 minutes will help keep food from sticking to it for several months at a time.

Glass - Everyday use

To rid drinking glasses of cloudiness or spots heat up a pot of equal parts of white distilled vinegar and water (use full-strength vinegar if your glasses are very cloudy), and let them soak in it for 15-30 minutes. Give them a good scrubbing with a bottle brush, then rinse clean.

Glass - Crystal and Fine Cut Glass

Add 225ml (1 cup) of white distilled vinegar to a basin of warm water. Gently dunk the glasses in the solution and allow to air-dry.

Glass ovenware

Fill ovenware with 1 part white distilled vinegar and 4 parts water and heat the mixture to a slow boil. Let it boil at a low level for five minutes. The stains should come off with some mild scrubbing once the mixture cools.

Grease Splatters

Remove grease splatters from all of your kitchen surfaces by washing them with a sponge dipped in undiluted white distilled vinegar. Use another sponge soaked in cold tap water to rinse, then wipe dry with a soft cloth.

Grease and food stains in saucepans (burnt-on)

Soften with a solution of 225ml (1 cup) apple cider vinegar and 2 tablespoons of sugar. Apply the mixture while the pan is still hot, and let it sit for an hour or so.

Grill Hoods/Extractor Fans

Use undiluted white distilled vinegar to cut through the grease on grill hoods and extractor fan covers.

Hob/Hotplate

Wipe with full strength white distilled vinegar to remove food stains.

Ice trays

To remove water spots or disinfect your trays, let them soak in undiluted white distilled vinegar for four to five hours, then rinse well under cold water and let dry.

Kettle

To remove limescale from your kettle, fill kettle with water and add 100ml (approx 1/2 cup) of white distilled vinegar. Let it stand overnight, then rinse well with clean water.

Microwave - General cleaning

To clean your microwave, place a glass bowl filled with a solution of 55ml (1/4 cup) vinegar in 225ml (1 cup water) inside the microwave and zap the mixture for five minutes on the highest setting. Once the bowl cools, dip a cloth or sponge into the liquid and use it to wipe away stains and splatters on the interior.

Microwave - Odour removal

Place 1 tablespoon of white wine vinegar in a microwave proof cup and heat in microwave to boiling, to elimate lingering odours.

Non-stick cookware

For mineral stains on your nonstick cookware, rub the utensil with a cloth dipped in undiluted white distilled vinegar. To loosen up stubborn stains, mix 2 tablespoons baking soda, 100ml (approx 1/2 cup) of white distilled vinegar, and 225ml (1 cup) of water and let it boil for 10 minutes.

Odours - Cooking Smells

Remove lingering cooking smells by filling a small bowl or cup full of undiluted distilled white vinegar, which will absorb unwanted odours.

Oven

Oven - General Cleaning

To remove grease and grime and cooking spills from inside your oven, make a paste of 225ml (1 cup) white distilled vinegar and 30g (1/4 cup) of powdered laundry detergent. Heat your oven for five minutes at 180 degrees and turn off. Spread the paste around the oven, applying it more heavily to very greasy areas. Leave paste on for an hour, then use a plastic spatula to gently scrape the dirt away.

Odours - Neutralize chemical odours

If you choose to clean your oven with chemical cleaners, keep your freshly-cleaned oven from stinking up your house next time you cook something, by wiping it with white distilled vinegar poured directly on the sponge as a final rinse. It neutralizes the harsh alkali of oven cleaners.

Oven - Odour removal

Stop unpleasant cooking odours from permeating through the house whilst cooking. Boil 225ml (1 cup) of white distilled vinegar with 450ml (2 cups) of water in a pan on the hob. Leave boiling until the liquid is almost gone.

Oven - Prevent build up of grease in Oven

Dip a sponge or cloth in full strength white distilled vinegar and wipe down all sides of the oven to prevent a greasy build up.

Refrigerator

Clean and disinfect by wiping with full strength white distilled vinegar to remove any potentially harmful bacteria.

Saucepans, skillets.

To remove stubborn stains, fill pan with equal parts of white distilled vinegar and water and bring to boil. Rinse thoroughly with clean water before use.

Scissors

When your scissor blades get sticky or grimy, don't use water to wash them off; you're far more likely to rust the fastener that holds the blades together - or the blades themselves - than get them clean. Instead, wipe down the blades with a cloth dipped in full-strength white distilled vinegar, and then dry with a rag or dish towel.

Stainless steel cookware

Soak in 450ml (2 cups) of white distilled vinegar for 30 minutes, then rinse with hot, soapy water followed by a cold-water rinse.

Stainless steel

To clean stainless steel fixtures around your home, apply a light misting of undiluted white vinegar from a recycled spray bottle. Buff with a soft cloth to bring out the brightness.

Tea Pot

Clean tea pots by boiling equal parts of white distilled vinegar and water for several minutes and let stand an hour. Then rinse with clean water.

Thermos flask

Fill with warm water and 50ml (approx. 1/4 cup) white distilled vinegar then add some uncooked rice, which will act as an abrasive. Close and shake well, then rinse and let it air-dry.

Vinyl Flooring

Add 100ml (approx 1/2 cup) of white distilled vinegar to a bucket of water to keep your vinyl floors clean. Not only does it keep the floors shiny but it kills the dust mites.

Washing-up liquid

Pour 3-4 tablespoons white distilled vinegar into your favourite brand (especially bargain brands) of washing-up liquid and give it a few shakes. The added vinegar will not only increase the detergent's grease-fighting capabilities, but also provide you with more dishwashing liquid for the money.

Waste disposal unit

Clean by running a tray of ice cubes with 55ml (1/4 cup) of white distilled vinegar poured over the ice.

Waxing Floors

When waxing a floor after scrubbing with a floor stripper, add 225ml (1 cup) of white distilled vinegar to rinse water. It neutralizes the chemicals and makes wax or floor finish adhere better.

Work Surface

Clean and disinfect by wiping with full strength white distilled vinegar.

Office

Before you start cleaning, make sure that all your equipment is shut off.

Mix a solution of equal parts water and white distilled vinegar. Moisten a cloth, then wring out any excess fluids, and use this to clean your home office equipment. It is essential that during the cleaning process you do not get any liquid on any part of the equipment, which will work better if you keep them clean and dust-free. The solution is suitable for cleaning:-

PC, Laptop, Screens, Copier, Scanner, Fax Machine, Calculator

Mouse

If you have a mouse with a removable tracking ball, use the same solution. First, remove the ball from underneath the mouse by twisting off the cover over it. Use a cloth, dampened with the solution and wrung out, to wipe the ball clean and to remove fingerprints and dirt from the mouse itself. Then use a moistened cotton swab to clean out the gunk and debris from inside the ball chamber (let it dry a couple of hours before reinserting the ball).

Bathroom

Bath
Clean thoroughly with a cloth or sponge dipped in full-strength white distilled vinegar, to ensure bacteria removal and extra shine. Rinse thoroughly with cold water.

Bath - Water marks
To remove hard-water stains pour in 675ml (3 cups) of distilled white vinegar under a running hot tap water. Allow the bathtub to fill up over the stains and allow it to soak for about four hours. When the water drains out, you should be able to easily scrub off the stains.

Bathroom Cabinet/Mirror
Clean and disinfect by wiping with a cloth dipped in white distilled vinegar.

Ceramic Tiles
Mix a solution of 1 part white distilled vinegar to 3 parts water and use a cloth to wipe tiles clean. This also preserves the colour of the grout.

Chrome fixtures
Apply a light misting of undiluted white vinegar from a recycled spray bottle. Buff with a soft cloth to bring out the brightness.

Grout
Dip an old toothbrush in undiluted white vinegar and scrub grout to remove grubbiness and restore to its original colour.

Hard water spots
To remove hard water spots from sinks, showers and baths, wipe using a cloth soaked in full-strength vinegar. Allow to stand for about five minutes and then rinse with clean water.

Jacuzzi
Pour about 4 1/2 litres of white distilled vinegar into the water about once a year and run it through. This will help keep the jets from clogging.

Limescale deposit

Heat a small container of white distilled vinegar to boiling point. Then pour over your fixtures that have deposits of limescale. This will release or remove the deposit.

Mould and mildew

Mix a solution of 3 tablespoons of white distilled vinegar, 1 teaspoon borax, and 450ml (2 cups) of hot water into a clean, recycled spray bottle and give it a few good shakes. Spray the solution onto the affected area and allow to soak in. For stubborn stains, use a soft scrubbing brush. Wipe away with a clean cloth. The solution is suitable for mould and mildew removal on painted surfaces, tiles, windows, or wherever you see mould or mildew spots.

Rinse cup

Fill with equal parts water and white distilled vinegar, or just full-strength vinegar, and let it sit overnight. Rinse thoroughly with cold water before using.

Shower curtain

Remove mildew from your shower curtain by placing it in your washing machine with a couple of towels. Add 110ml (1/2 cup) of liquid laundry detergent and 115g (1/2 cup) of baking soda to the load, and wash it in warm water on your machine's regular cycle. Add 225ml (1 cup) white distilled vinegar to the first rinse. Before the machine goes into the spin cycle, remove the curtain and let it hang-dry.

Shower doors - glass

Wipe with a cloth dipped in a solution of 110ml (1/2 cup) of white distilled vinegar, 225ml (1 cup) of ammonia, and 60g (1/4 cup) of baking soda mixed in about 4 litres of warm water.

Shower door - tracks

Fill the tracks with approximately 450ml (2 cups) of full-strength white vinegar and let it sit for three to five hours. If the tracks are really dirty, heat the vinegar in a glass container for 30 seconds in your microwave first. Then pour some hot water over the track to flush away the gunk.

Shower heads - removable

Remove blockages and mineral deposits from showerheads by placing them in 1 litre of boiling water with 110ml (1/2 cup) white distilled vinegar for 10 minutes (use hot, not boiling, liquid for plastic showerheads).

Shower heads - fixed

If you have a non-removable shower head, fill a small plastic bag half full with white distilled vinegar and tape it over the fixture. Let it sit for about 1 hour, then remove the bag and wipe off any remaining vinegar from the showerhead.

Sink - Porcelain

Clean thoroughly with a cloth or sponge dipped in full-strength white distilled vinegar, to ensure bacteria removal and extra shine. Rinse thoroughly with cold water.

Sink - Porcelain, water marks

To remove hard-water stains pour in 225ml (1 cup) of white distilled vinegar under running hot tap water. Allow the sink to fill up over the stains and allow it to soak for about four hours. When the water drains out, you should be able to easily scrub off the stains.

Soap build-up

To remove soap scum and build up from sinks, showers and baths, wipe with a cloth soaked in full-strength vinegar. Allow to stand for about five minutes and then rinse with clean water.

Soap dish

Get the grime and soap build up out of the grooves of your soap dish by cleaning with a cloth moistened with white distilled vinegar.

Taps

Remove grime and dirt that builds up around the base of taps by soaking paper towels in full-strength white distilled vinegar and then wrap the towels around the fixtures. Leave for about an hour and then remove towels and clean as usual.

Toilet bowl

Pour 450ml (2 cups) of white distilled vinegar into the bowl and let the solution soak overnight before flushing. This will also remove water rings that typically appear just above the water level.

Toothbrush holder

Get the grime and caked-on toothpaste drippings out of the grooves by cleaning with a cloth moistened with white distilled vinegar.

Towel Rack

Clean and disinfect by wiping with a cloth dipped in white distilled vinegar.

Furniture

Cupboard - musty odour

Remove the contents then wash with a cloth dampened in a solution of 225ml (1 cup) each of white distilled vinegar and ammonia and 60g (1/4 cup) of baking soda in 4 litres of water. Leave doors open to dry completely.

Fireplaces

Create an equal part mix of water and white distilled vinegar to remove the blackened soot on glass front doors. If the doors have a spring-loaded clip, remove it, then take out the doors. Lay them flat on newspapers, spray with the vinegar/water solution and soak. Wipe it off with newspaper.

Leather sofas and chairs

Make a cleaning solution from equal parts of white distilled vinegar and boiled linseed oil in a recycled spray bottle. Shake the bottle well and spray lightly and evenly over your furniture. Rub it off with a clean cloth.

Leather sofas and chairs - watermarks and water rings

Moisten a sponge with white distilled vinegar and dab gently, ensuring that you completely cover the area affected by the mark.

Wood furniture - scratches

Conceal scratches by mixing some white distilled vinegar and iodine in a small jar and paint over the scratch with a small artist's brush. Use more iodine for darker woods; more vinegar for lighter shades.

Wood furniture - water rings

To remove white rings left by wet glasses on wood furniture, mix equal parts white distilled vinegar and olive oil and apply it with a soft cloth while moving with the wood grain. Use another clean, soft cloth to shine it up.

Wood furniture - wax and polish build-up

To remove built-up wax and polish dip a cloth in equal parts white distilled vinegar and water and squeeze it out well. Then, moving with the grain, clean away the polish.

Blinds - Venetian or slatted

Put on a white cotton glove and moisten the fingers in a solution made of equal parts white vinegar and hot tap water. Now simply slide your fingers across both sides of each slat and prepare to be amazed. Use a container of clean water to periodically wash off the glove.

Brickwork

Wipe with a damp mop dipped in 225ml (1 cup) of white vinegar mixed with approximately 4 litres of warm water. You can also use this same solution to brighten up the bricks around your fireplace.

Walls and Woodwork

You can ease the job of washing painted walls and woodwork by using a mixture of 225ml (1 cup) ammonia, 110ml (1/2 cup) white distilled or cider vinegar and 60g (1/4 cup) of baking soda with about 4 litres of warm water. Wipe this solution over walls or blinds with a sponge or cloth and rinse with clean water.

Windows

Simply wash with a mixture of equal parts of white distilled vinegar and warm water. Dry with a soft cloth. This solution will make your windows gleam and will not leave the usual film or streaks on the glass.

Wood panelling - revitalize

Mix 1 pint of warm water, 4 tablespoons of white or apple cider vinegar, and 2 tablespoons olive oil in a container, give it a couple of shakes, and apply with a clean cloth. Let the mixture soak into the wood for several minutes, then polish with a dry cloth

Brass, Bronze and Copper

Clean brass, bronze, copper objects and doorware by making a paste of equal parts distilled white vinegar and salt, or vinegar and baking soda (wait for the fizzing to stop before using). Use a clean, soft cloth or paper towel to rub the paste into the item until the tarnish is gone. Then rinse with cool water and polish with a soft towel until dry.

Mirrors

To make a homemade anti-fogging glass cleaner suitable for mirrors and glassware, place 1 part white distilled vinegar to 3 parts water in a spray bottle and mist. Wipe with a soft lint free cloth.

Piano Keys

Remove grimy fingerprints and stains off piano keys. Dip a soft cloth into a solution of 110ml (1/2 cup) distilled white vinegar mixed in 2 cups water. Squeeze it out until there are no drips, then gently wipe off each key. Use a second cloth to dry off the keys as you move along, then leave the keyboard uncovered for 24 hours.

Silver

Make your silverware - as well as your pure silver bracelets, rings, and other jewellery - shine like new by soaking them in a mixture of 110ml (1/2 cup) of white distilled vinegar and 2 tablespoons of baking soda for two to three hours. Rinse them under cold water and dry thoroughly with a soft cloth.

Carpets and Rugs

Carpets and Rugs - Mildew

Prevent mildew from forming on the bottoms of rugs and carpeting by misting the backs with full-strength white vinegar from a spray bottle.

Restore your rugs

If your rugs or carpets are looking worn and dingy from too much foot traffic bring them back to life by brushing them with a clean broom dipped in a solution of 225ml (1 cup) of distilled white vinegar in 4 litres of water. Your faded threads will perk up, and you don't even need to rinse off the solution.

Spot stain remover

Fill a trigger spray bottle with one part distilled white vinegar to five parts water. Take a second spray bottle and fill with one part white, non sudsy amonnia and five parts water. Saturate stain with vinegar solution. Let dwell for a few minutes and blot thoroughly with a clean cloth. Then go over the area with the ammonia solution, let dwell and blot again. Repeat until the stain is gone.

Stain remover

Rub light carpet stains with a mixture of 2 tablespoons of salt dissolved in 110ml (1/2 cup) of white vinegar. Let the solution dry, then vacuum. For larger or darker stains, add 2 tablespoons borax to the mixture and use in the same way. For tough, ground-in dirt and other stains, make a paste of 1 tablespoon vinegar with 1 tablespoon cornflour and rub it into the stain using a dry cloth. Let it set for two days, then vacuum.

Stain and Odour removal

Air freshener

Mix 1 teaspoon of baking soda, 1 tablespoon of distilled white vinegar and 450ml (2 cups of water). After it stops foaming, mix well, and spritz into the air using a spray bottle.

Ballpoint-pen marks

Dab some full-strength distilled white vinegar on the ballpoint pen mark using a cloth or a sponge. Repeat until the marks are gone.

Candle wax

To remove candle wax first soften the wax using a blow-dryer on its hottest setting and blot up as much as you can with paper towels. Then remove what's left by rubbing with a cloth soaked in a solution made of equal parts distilled white vinegar and water. Wipe clean with a soft, absorbent cloth.

Chewing gum

Remove chewing gum from textiles by saturating the area in distilled white vinegar. Heat the vinegar first, either in the microwave or on the hob, and this will make it will work faster.

Deodorize footlockers, car boots and other enclosed spaces

Soak a slice of white bread in white vinegar and leave it in the malodorous space overnight. The smell should be gone by morning.

Glue - Acetate, Fiberglass, Rayon, Silk, Triacetate, Wool

Immediately sponge the area with water. Then apply a wet spotter and a few drops of white vinegar. To prepare a wet spotter, mix 1 part glycerine, 1 part white dishwashing detergent, and 8 parts water. Shake well before each use. Store wet spotter in a plastic squeeze bottle. Cover with an absorbent pad dampened with wet spotter. Let it stand as long as any stain is being picked up. Change the pad as it removes the stain. Keep both the stain and pad moist with wet spotter and vinegar. Repeat until no more stain is removed.

Rust

For rust stains and hard water deposits apply vinegar full-strength until spot disappears, then rinse. Repeat if necessary.

Smoke odour

Remove lingering smoky odour by placing a shallow bowl about three quarters full of white or cider vinegar in the room where the scent is strongest. Use several bowls if the smell permeates your entire home. The odour should be gone in less than a day.

Stickers

To remove a sticker affixed to painted furniture or a painted wall, simply saturate the corners and sides of the sticker with full-strength white vinegar and carefully scrape it off (using an expired credit card or a plastic phone card). Remove any sticky remains by pouring on a bit more vinegar. Let it sit for a minute or two, and then wipe with a clean cloth. This approach is equally effective for removing price tags and other stickers from glass, plastic, and other glossy surfaces.

DIY

Air-conditioner and humidifier filters
An air-conditioner or humidifier filter can quickly become inundated with dust, soot and even potentially harmful bacteria. Every 10 days or so, clean your filter with equal parts white distilled vinegar and warm water. Let the filter soak in the solution for an hour, then simply squeeze it dry before using. If your filters are particularly dirty, let them soak overnight.

Concrete - handcare after use
Even though you wear rubber gloves when working with concrete, some of the stuff inevitably splashes on your skin. Prolonged contact with wet concrete can cause your skin to crack, and may even lead to eczema. Use undiluted white distilled vinegar to wash dried concrete or mortar off your skin, then wash with warm, soapy water.

Fixings - Loosening
Pour white distilled vinegar on rusted hinges and screws to loosen them up for removal.

Painting
To achieve the best results for your paintwork, it is essential to remove all dust and grime so simply wipe over with a cloth moistened with a solution made from 1 part white distilled vinegar to 3 parts water. Allow to dry before beginning to paint.

Paint - Removal from glass
Hot vinegar can be used to remove paint from glass. Just heat up the white distilled vinegar either in a microwave or on the hob and use a cloth to wipe away paint.

Painting - Cement floors
Painted cement floors have a tendency to peel after a while. But you can keep the paint stuck to the cement longer by giving the floor an initial coat of white distilled vinegar before you paint it. Wait until the vinegar has dried, then begin painting.

Painting - Metal

Wiping down clean metal surfaces with a vinegar solution made of 1 part white distilled vinegar to 5 parts water prepares the surface for painting, and reduces the incidence of peeling.

Paint Brushes - Softening

Bring a pan of white distilled vinegar to the boil on the hob and allow brushes to simmer for around 5 minutes. Remove from the pan and wash in hot soapy water.

Paint fumes

Place a couple of shallow dishes filled with undiluted white distilled vinegar around a freshly painted room to quickly get rid of the strong paint smell.

Paint - Tempera

Dip a cloth or sponge in full-strength white distilled vinegar and then simply wipe away paint.

Plaster

If you add a couple of teaspoons of white distilled vinegar to your plaster mix, this will allow you more time to work the plaster before it hardens.

Radiators - Cleaning the vent

Turn down the thermostat. Unscrew the air vent, soak it in white distilled vinegar to clean it, then turn the thermostat all the way up. After a few minutes, you'll hear a hissing sound followed by a little bit of water spurting out. Finally, steam will start exiting that hole. Turn off the radiator valve and replace the vent. It should be straight up and hand tight. You should not need or use a wrench.

Remove glue from furniture joints

To loosen old glue from around the rungs and joints of tables and chairs you are repairing or renovating, apply full-strength white distilled vinegar directly onto the joint.

Reviving an old stove or fireplace

Ensure the stove or fireplace is cold and dust and rust free by cleaning thoroughly with a cloth or brush dipped in white distilled vinegar. Create a creamy paste using blacklead and white distilled vinegar, then apply to all metal areas. Buff to a shine with a stiff brush and soft cloth.

Rust - Removal

To remove rust from bolts and other metals, soak them in full strength white distilled vinegar.

Rust - reviving old tools

If you want to clean up those rusted old tools you recently unearthed in your garage or picked up at a boot sale, soak them in full-strength white distilled vinegar for several days to remove rust, dirt and grime.

Varnished Wood

A "cloudy" appearance on varnished wood can be removed easily, assuming the cloudiness hasn't permeated through to the wood, by rubbing the surface with a cloth moistened with a solution of 1 tablespoon of white distilled vinegar and 1 litre of warm water. Ensure that there is no excess moisture on the cloth by wringing out thoroughly before use, and then complete the job by drying the surface with a soft cloth or rag.

Wallpaper - Removal

Spray white distilled vinegar directly onto the surface of the wallpaper and leave for a few minutes, then try removing the paper with a scraper. If it won't shift that easily try scoring the paper then spray again. Spray the wall again and scrape the excess glue off the wall. Wipe remaining glue off with vinegar and rinse with water.

Woodstain

White distilled vinegar can be mixed with water-based inks to make a simple stain for wood. Pour vinegar into a mixing jar, add the ink until the desired colour is achieved and apply to wood with a brush or rag.

Car care

Car carpets and floor mats

A good vacuuming will get up the sand and other loose debris from your car's carpeting, but it won't remove stains or ground-in dirt. For that, mix up a solution of equal parts water and white vinegar and sponge it into the carpet. Give the mixture a couple of minutes to settle in; then blot it up with a cloth or paper towel. This technique will also eliminate salt residues left on car carpets during the winter months.

Fingermarks and handprints

Remove unwanted fingermarks and handprints from the interior of your car by wiping with a cloth mixed with equal parts white distilled vinegar and water.

Odours - Vomit and other unpleasant smells in your car

To get rid of these smells place a bowl of white distilled vinegar on the floor of the car, close it up for the night. Remember to remove the bowl prior to beginning a journey.

Preventing ice on your windscreen

Mix 3 parts white distilled vinegar to 1 part water and coat the windows with this solution. This vinegar and water combination will keep your windscreens ice and frost-free.

Remove car stickers

Saturate the top and sides of the sticker with undiluted white distilled vinegar and wait 10-15 minutes for the vinegar to soak through. Then use an expired credit card (or used telephone card) to scrape it off. Use more full-strength vinegar to get rid of any remaining gluey residue. Use the same technique to detach those cute stickers your kids used to decorate the back window!

Windscreen wiper blades

When your windscreen actually gets blurrier after you turn on your wipers during a rainstorm, it usually means that your wiper blades are dirty. To make them as good as new, dampen a cloth or rag with some full-strength white distilled vinegar and run it down the full length of each blade.

Outdoor/Gardening

Animal deterrent

Some animals (including cats, deer, dogs, rabbits, foxes and raccoons) dislike the scent of vinegar even after it has dried. You can keep these unauthorized visitors out of your garden by soaking several recycled rags in full-strength white distilled vinegar, and placing them on stakes around your garden, particularly around areas such as vegetable patches and flower beds. Resoak the rags approximately every 7-10 days.

Antibacterial hand spray - prevent infection

If you prefer not to wear gloves while gardening — carry a spray bottle with white distilled vinegar with you and if you scratch yourself, spray it with the solution straight away which should prevent infection.

Bird droppings

Remove bird droppings by spraying them with full-strength apple cider vinegar. Or pour the vinegar onto a rag and wipe them off.

Bird nests

Use vinegar to deter birds building their mud nests in your facias. When you see that they are interested in building where they are not wanted, drench the area with full-strength white distilled vinegar. They will probably try several more times to make a nest. Keep spraying the area with vinegar as they become discouraged after several attempts and go elsewhere. Under no circumstances spray the birds.

Brickwork - remove calcium

To get rid of calcium buildup on brick or on limestone, use a spray bottle with half white distilled vineger and half water, then just let it set. The solution will do all the work.

Cantaloupes

Keep mould at bay whilst waiting for your cantaloupes to ripen by rubbing each melon with approximately 1 teaspoonful of full-strength white distilled vinegar.

Climbing frame

Clean and disinfect regularly by washing with a solution of 1 part white distilled vinegar and 1 part water.

Concrete - drives and pathways

Remove stains and unsightly marks by pouring full-strength white distilled vinegar over the area. Repeat as necessary until stain fades.

Decking

Mix a solution of 225ml (1 cup) of ammonia, 110ml (1/2 cup) of white vinegar, and 60g (1/2 cup) of baking soda mixed in 4 litres of water. Use a bristle brush or broom dipped in the solution and brush onto the deck to remove mildew.

Drains

To "green clean" your drains without the use of harsh chemicals, pour 60g (1/2 cup) of baking soda and 110ml (1/2 cup) of white distilled vinegar down the drain and then cover whilst the solution fizzes. Follow this with a bucket of very hot or boiling water.

Flower pots - stain removal from clay and plastic flowerpots

Create a solution of 1 part white distilled vinegar and 2 parts cold water and soak pots until they look clean and new (sometimes takes an hour). Wash with soap and water before reusing.

Fresh cut flowers

Keep cut flowers fresh longer (or even perk up droopy ones) by adding two tablespoons of white distilled vinegar and one tablespoon of sugar to the vase of water.

Garden Furniture - cane and wicker

Sponge furniture with a solution of 1 part white distilled vinegar and 1 part hot water. Place the chairs out in the hot sun to dry and this will clean and improve the appearance of sagging.

Garden Furniture - mesh and umbrellas

To deodorize and inhibit mildew growth on outdoor plastic mesh furniture and patio umbrellas, mix 450ml (2 cups) of white vinegar and 2 tablespoons of liquid detergent in a bucket of hot water. Use a soft brush to work it into the grooves of the plastic as well as for scrubbing seat pads and umbrella fabric. Rinse with cold water; then dry in the sun.

Garden Furniture - plastic

Spray with full-strength white vinegar and wipe with a cloth. This will remove dirt build up and mildew and the vinegar should prevent the mildew reappearing for a while.

Garden Furniture - wood

Mix a solution of 225ml (1 cup) of ammonia, 110ml (1/2 cup) of white vinegar, and 60g (1/2 cup) of baking soda mixed in 4 litres of water. Soak a sponge or rag in the solution and wipe down the furniture to remove mildew.

Greenhouse glass

Mix 3 tablespoons of white distilled vinegar with 1/2 teaspoon of liquid detergent and 575ml (1 pint) of water and decant into a trigger spray bottle. Lightly mist the glass and then wipe dry with a paper towel and polish with newspaper for a fantastic shine. This solution works on all glass surfaces.

Insects - fixed trap

If the bugs are feasting on the fruits and vegetables in your garden, fill a 2 litre plastic bottle with 225ml (1 cup) of apple cider vinegar and 120g (1 cup) of sugar. Next, slice up a banana peel into small pieces and put these into the bottle with 225ml (1 cup) of cold water and shake it up. Tie a piece of string around the neck of the bottle and hang it from a low tree branch, or place it on the ground, to trap and kill insects. Replace used traps with new ones as needed.

Insects - portable trap

If you are hosting a barbecue or party in the garden and want to ensure that your guests are not plagued by flying insects (gnats, flies, mosquitoes etc) place a bowl filled with apple cider vinegar near some food, but away from you and your guests. By the evening's end, most of your uninvited guests will be floating inside the bowl.

Insect repellant

If you have problems with ants and other insects invading your home, they are probably crossing your door and/or window sills and baseboards. Pour full-strength white distilled vinegar around these areas and this will prevent the insects invading - for some reason, they will not cross it!

Lawns - brown patches

If your lawn suffers from brown patches caused by dog urine, place a few drops of white distilled vinegar in your dog's water bowl every day and this will neutralize the acidity in the urine and lessen the likelihood of brown patches appearing. Alternatively if you catch your dog "in the act", mix a solution of equal parts white distilled vinegar and water and spray this liberally over the area where your dog has been which should help.

Lawn mower blades

Grass, especially when it's damp, has a tendency to accumulate on your lawn mower blades after you cut the lawn. Wipe down the blades with a cloth dampened with undiluted white distilled vinegar. It will clean off leftover grass on the blades, as well as any insects.

Patios, Paths and Driveways - dandelions and unwanted grass

Spray the unwanted weeds with full-strength white distilled vinegar or apple cider vinegar. Give each plant a single spritz of vinegar in its midsection, or in the middle of the flower before the plants go to seed. Aim another shot near the stem at ground level so the vinegar can soak down to the roots. Keep an eye on the weather, though; if it rains the next day, you'll need to give the weeds another spraying.

Pesticide - Slugs

If you have a slug problem, drop a few drops (an eye dropper works well) of white distilled vinegar on them and they will dissolve. But be careful not to get the vinegar on plants, it will kill them.

Pesticide - Mealybugs

These are the most insidious and common pests on both houseplants and in the garden. Stop the invasion by dabbing the insects with a cotton swab dipped in full-strength white distilled vinegar which will kill the insects and any eggs left behind.

Plant diseases - rust, black spot, and powdery mildew

Mix 2 tablespoons of apple cider vinegar in 2 litres of water, and pour some into a recycled spray bottle. Spray the solution on your affected plants in the morning or early evening (when temperatures are relatively cool and there's no direct light on the plant) until the condition is cured.

Plant diseases - yellow leaves on plants

The sudden appearance of yellow leaves on plants accustomed to acidic soils-such as azaleas, hydrangeas, and gardenias-could signal a drop in the plant's iron intake or a shift in the ground's pH. Either problem can be resolved by watering the soil around the afflicted plants once a week for three weeks with 225ml (1 cup) of a solution made by mixing 2 tablespoons of apple cider vinegar in 1 litre of water.

Sand Pit - Cat repellant

Pour full-strength white distilled vinegar around the children's sand pit to keep cats from using it as their litter box. Reapply every two months.

Seed germination

You can get woody seeds, such as moonflower, passionflower, morning glory, and gourds, off to a healthier start by lightly rubbing them between a couple of sheets of fine sandpaper and soaking them overnight in a solution of 110ml (1/2 cup) of apple cider vinegar and 1/2 litre (1 pint) warm water. Next morning, remove the seeds from the solution, rinse them off, and plant them. You can also use the solution (minus the sandpaper treatment) to start many herb and vegetable seeds.

Skincare

If you have been working in the garden without gloves, rinse your hands with white distilled vinegar and then wash as normal. This will avoid rough and flaky skin, particuarly if you have been working with garden lime.

Slide - plastic

Clean and disinfect regularly by washing with a solution of 1 part white distilled vinegar and 1 part water.

Soil

If you have alkaline soil and are trying to grow rhododendrons, gardenias,azaleas or other acid loving plants, add 1 1/2 tablespoons of white distilled vinegar to 2 litres of water, and water thoroughly.

Soil - acidity test

To do a quick test for excess acidity in your soil place a handful of earth in a container and then pour in 110ml (1/2 cup) of white distilled vinegar and 60g (1/2 cup) of baking soda. If the soil fizzes or bubbles, it is definitely acidic.

Soil - alkalinity test

To do a quick test for excess alkalinity in your soil place a handful of earth in a container and then pour in 110ml (1/2 cup) of white distilled vinegar. If the soil fizzes or bubbles, it is definitely alkaline.

Swimming Pool

Pour full-strength white distilled vinegar around the sides of your pool and it helps keeps flies away.

Swings

Clean and disinfect regularly by washing the seat with a solution of 1 part white distilled vinegar and 1 part water.

Wendy House

Keep the wendy house clean and bug free by washing regularly with a mix of 1 part white distilled vinegar and 1 part water.

Tree House

Douse the outside of the tree house with white distilled vinegar to keep cats from using it as a kitty house!

Cookery

Basil and Garlic Vinegar

900ml/4 cups red wine vinegar
1 cup fresh basil
8 cloves garlic, crushed

1. Rinse and dry basil thoroughly then place in jar and add the crushed garlic cloves.
Pour in vinegar and cap with sterile lids. Let jars stand for about a month in the sun,
turning occasionally.

2. Add fresh wine vinegar if necessary to keep herbs covered. May be kept for about
3 to 4 months at room temperature.

Blackberry Vinegar

450g/16oz blackberries
450ml/2 cups white wine vinegar
1 tbsp sugar

1. Place the berries in a glass jar and sprinkle with sugar. Stir for one minute to
release a bit of the juice. Pour the white wine vinegar over the berries, cap the jar
and let it sit on a cool, dark shelf for 3-4 weeks.

2. Pour the mixture through a fine strainer to remove the berries' flesh and seeds.

Champagne Vinegar

To make homemade champagne vinegar, store leftover champagne in an open,
widemouthed jar at room temperature. In a few weeks, it will turn into vinegar.

Chilli Vinegar

20-25 chillies roughly chopped
565ml/2 1/2 cups white wine vinegar or white malt vinegar

1. Bring vinegar to the boil, add chillies and return to the boil. Pour into a wide
mouthed jar, and leave to stand in a sunny window for 5-6 weeks. Strain through
muslin, pour into sterilised bottles and seal as you would pickles.

Cranberry Vinegar

450ml/2 cups cider vinegar
30g/1/4 cup cranberries, crushed slightly

1. Bring the vinegar to a boil. Put the cranberries in a sterilized jar. Pour the vinegar over. Allow the mixture to cool to room temperature, then seal and place in a cool place for 15 days.

2. Filter the vinegar through a cheesecloth or paper coffee filter into decorative jars.

Fennel Vinegar

450ml/2 cups white wine vinegar or cider vinegar
1-1/2 tbsps crushed fennel seeds

1. Bring the vinegar to a boil. Put the fennel in a sterilized jar. Pour the vinegar over. Allow the mixture to cool to room temperature, then seal and place in a cool place for 15 days. Filter the vinegar through a cheesecloth or paper coffee filter into decorative jars.

Jalapeno and Garlic Vinegar

450ml/2 cups white wine vinegar or cider vinegar
2 jalapeno peppers
2 garlic cloves, crushed

1. Cut small slits into the peppers and place in a clean jar with the crushed garlic. Heat the vinegar to just below boiling point and then pour over the peppers and garlic. Seal the jar and allow to stand for 3-4 weeks in a cool dark place or until desired strength is achieved. Line a colander or strainer with cheesecloth over a container and drain vinegar from the peppers. Decant into dry, clean bottles.

Mediterranean Herb Vinegar

450ml/2 cups cider or red wine vinegar
1-1/2 tsps oregano or other mediterranean herb
1/4 tsp garlic powder

1. Combine ingredients in a saucepan; bring to a boil. Remove from heat and let cool slightly. Pour into a 1-pint jar or bottle. Cover and shake. Let stand for at least 1 week before using. Strain and refrigerate.

Pomegranate Vinegar

115g/1 cup pomegranate seeds
450ml/2 cups white wine vinegar

1. Place pomegranate seeds in a dry sterilized jar. Top with the vinegar. Seal jar with a tight-fitting lid. Place in full sunlight (a sunny window works well). Let stand 8 to 10 days or until desired strength is achieved.

2. Line a colander or strainer with cheesecloth over a container and drain vinegar from pomegranate seeds. Decant into dry, clean bottles. Seal and store bottles in a cool, dark place. Store up to six months.

Raspberry Vinegar

450ml/2 cups white wine vinegar
225g/1/2 lb raspberries
1 tbsp fine sugar

1. Bring the vinegar to a boil. Crush the raspberries and pour a little of the boiling vinegar on them to thin. Put the crushed raspberries in a wide mouth, sterilized jar. Add the sugar and the rest of the vinegar. Allow the mixture to cool to room temperature, then seal and place in a cool place for 10 days.

2. Filter the vinegar through a cheesecloth or paper coffee filter into decorative jars. Slide 2 or 3 whole raspberries into the bottles. Keep stored in a cool, dark place.

Spiced Vinegar

450ml/2 cups white wine vinegar
1/2 tsp each: whole cloves; whole allspice; mustard seed; and celery seed
1/2 tbsp sugar
1/2 tsp salt
1 tbsp brandy

1. Bring the vinegar to a boil. Crush the spices lightly. Put the spices, sugar, salt and brandy in a sterilized jar. Pour the vinegar over the spices.

2. Allow the mixture to cool to room temperature, then seal and place in a cool place for 15 days. Filter the vinegar through a cheesecloth or paper coffee filter into decorative jars.

Strawberry Vinegar

450g/16oz strawberries, hulled and sliced
450ml/2 cups white wine vinegar
2 tbsps sugar

1. In a bowl stir together the strawberries, the vinegar, and the sugar and let the mixture stand, covered, at room temperature for 2 days. Discard the strawberries with a slotted spoon and strain the vinegar through a fine sieve lined with a triple thickness of rinsed and squeezed cheesecloth into a bowl.

2. Transfer the vinegar to a bottle with a tight-fitting lid and use it in salad dressings and marinades. The vinegar keeps in a dark, cool place indefinitely.

Tarragon Vinegar

450ml/2 cups white wine vinegar
1 cloves garlic, peeled
5 black peppercorns
5 mustard seeds
1/2 cup fresh tarragon
Few branches of tarragon for decoration

1. In a large sterilized jar, put the garlic, peppercorns, mustard and tarragon. Bring the vinegar to a boil and pour it over the aromatics. Close tightly and store in a cool place for 15 days, shaking occasionally.

2. Filter the vinegar through coffee filters or cheesecloth into a new, sterilized bottle. Slide a branch or two of the tarragon into the strained vinegar.

Balsamic Vinaigrette

1 tbsp olive oil
200ml/scant cup of vegetable oil
2 tbsps red wine vinegar
2 tbsps balsamic vinegar
1 1/2 tbsps light brown sugar
Salt and pepper

1. Combine all of the ingredients in a screwtop jar and shake until the sugar has dissolved. Use on fresh, baby greens or on a pear/Roquefort/spring green salad.

Blue Cheese & Mustard Vinaigrette

3 tbsps chicken stock
75g/3 oz. crumbled roquefort
1 egg yolk
1-1/2 tbsps Dijon mustard
1 tbsp white wine vinegar
1 tsp packed brown sugar (light or dark)
60ml/1/4 cup olive oil
1 tbsp chopped chives
salt and freshly ground pepper

1. Pour the stock into a small bowl and heat in the microwave about 45 seconds. Stir the stock and the cheese together to make a smooth paste. Place the cheese in a blender. Add the egg, mustard, vinegar and sugar.

2. Blend the ingredients and with the motor running, add the olive oil in a slow, thin stream. Pour the mixture into a bowl and stir in the chives. Taste and adjust the seasonings. If the mixture it too thick, thin with additional stock. The dressing may be stored covered in the refrigerator for up to 5 days.

3. May be used to dress a simple green salad or used as a dip for a platter of crudités or buffalo wings. Drizzle on some roasted asparagus.

Warm Vinaigrette with Cassis

75ml/1/3 cup walnut or hazelnut oil
3 shallots, minced
75ml/1/3 cup vegetable oil
2 tbsps red wine vinegar
1 tbsp freshly squeezed lemon juice
55ml/1/4 cup crème de cassis
1 tbsp honey
Sea salt & freshly ground pepper

1. Heat half of the walnut oil in a small saucepan over medium heat. Add the shallots and cook 5 minutes. Reduce the heat to low, add the remaining walnut oil, vegetable oil, vinegar, lemon juice, cassis and honey. If using immediately, keep it warm before dressing your salad. Or it may be made ahead and kept for 1 week in the refrigerator. Reheat before using.

Champagne Vinaigrette

2 tsps Dijon mustard
55ml/1/4 cup champagne vinegar
165ml/3/4 cup extra-virgin olive oil
1/2 tsp salt
Pinch of freshly ground black pepper

1. Combine the mustard and vinegar; whisk together and while whisking constantly, then slowly drizzle in olive oil. Season with salt and pepper.

Classic Vinaigrette

4 tbsps olive oil
1 tbsp cider, wine or balsamic vinegar
1 tbsp lemon juice
1 large clove of garlic, crushed
1 large pinch of mustard
Salt and pepper

1. Combine all of the ingredients in a screwtop jar and shake well. This classic recipe can form the basis of many vinaigrettes. There are endless combinations of ingredients that can be used. The best thing to do is to experiment and find your own unique flavour!

Vinaigrette with Gherkins, Shallots and Capers

1 tbsps wine vinegar
5 tbsps olive oil
1/8 tsp dried mustard
Small glove garlic, pressed
1 tsp finely chopped shallot
1 tsp finely chopped capers
1 tsp finely chopped gherkins
2 tbsps chopped fresh herbs (parsley, tarrogon, chives, chervil)
1/4 tsp salt

1. Combine all of the ingredients in a screwtop jar and shake for about a minute.

Lemon Dill Vinaigrette

110ml/1/2 cup fresh lemon juice
2 tbsps Dijon mustard
400ml/1-3/4 cups olive oil
1/2 cup chopped fresh dill
Salt & freshly ground pepper

1. Whisk the lemon juice and mustard together. Gradually whisk in the oil, and then the dill. Season with salt and pepper and allow to stand at room temperature for several hours to allow the flavours to infuse.

Lemon & Leek Vinaigrette

1 egg yolk
2 tbsps Dijon mustard
3 tbsps tarragon vinegar
1 leek, well rinsed, white bulk & light green stalk finely minced
3 tbsps dried tarragon
340ml/1-1/2 cups vegetable oil
225ml/1 cup extra virgin olive oil
Salt & freshly ground pepper

1. Whisk the egg yolk and mustard together. Whisk in the lemon juice and vinegar. Mix in the tarragon and the leek until combined. Whisking constantly, pour in the oils in a slow, steady stream. Season with salt and pepper.

Vinaigrette with Lemon Juice, Garlic and Mint

3 tbsps freshly squeezed lemon juice
Salt and freshly ground pepper
110ml/1/2 cup olive oil
1 whole garlic clove, put through a press
3 tbsps chopped fresh mint

1. Pour the lemon juice into a bowl and mix in the salt and pepper so that the lemon juice will begin to dissolve the salt.

2. Whisk in the olive oil and continue whisking until the dressing turns opaque. Add the garlic and the mint. This dressing is well suited to a crisp lettuce like romaine.

Mango Vinaigrette

1 mango, peeled
Grated zest and juice of 1 lime
1 tbsp chopped fresh corriander
1 tbsp sugar
75ml/1/3 cup seasoned rice wine vinegar
1 tsp honey mustard
225ml/1 cup vegetable oil or light olive oil
Salt and freshly ground black pepper to taste

1. Cut the mango flesh away from the pit and chop the mango coarsely. Place the mango and all the remaining ingredients, except the oil, salt, and pepper, in a blender or food processor and puree.

2. With the machine running, drizzle in the oil. Add the salt and pepper. Store in an airtight container in the refrigerator for up to 3 weeks.

Vinaigrette with Orange

Juice of 2 oranges
1/2 tsp finely grated orange peel
2 tbsps balsamic vinegar
2 tbsps white wine vinegar
1 shallot, very finely chopped
Salt & freshly ground pepper
60ml/1/4 cup corn oil
60ml/1/2 cup hazelnut oil
1 tbsp chopped fresh tarragon leaves

1. Put the orange juice and zest in a small saucepan and reduce by three quarters over high heat.

2. Pour the orange juice reduction into a bowl and blend in the vinegars, shallot, salt and pepper. Whisk in the oil and tarragon.

Pink Peppercorn Vinaigrette

1 tbsp red wine vinegar
2 tbsps fresh lemon juice
3 tbsps olive oil
2 small shallots, very thinly sliced
2 tbsps pink peppercorns, slightly crushed
Freshly ground pepper
1/2 cup flat leaf parsley, finely chopped

1. Whisk the vinegar, lemon juice and olive oil together. Add the chopped parsley and pink peppercorns. Season to taste with salt and pepper.

Warm Port Vinaigrette

3 shallots, minced
565ml/2-1/2 cups extra virgin olive oil
110ml/1/2 cup port
55ml/1/4 cup balsamic vinaigrette
2-1/2 tbsps honey
2 tbsps fresh lemon juice
Salt & freshly ground pepper

1. Place the shallots in a skillet, pour the oil over them and heat over med-high heat until it starts to sizzle. Reduce heat and simmer 2 minutes, remove from heat.

2. Whisk port, vinegar, honey and lemon juice together. Whisk in hot shallot/oil mixture and season with salt & pepper.

Tomato Vinaigrette

450g/1 lb cherry tomatoes
1 tbsp pastis (Pernod or Richard)
5 tbsps olive oil
1 tbsp sherry vinegar
1-3 drops hot sauce (Tabasco)
1 tsp sugar

1. In a food processor, combine the tomatoes, pastis, vinegar, olive oil, sugar, hot sauce, salt and pepper and blend until puréed.

Apple Balsamic Syrup
Apple juice concentrate
Balsamic vinegar

1, Combine equal amounts of defrosted apple juice concentrate and balsamic
vinegar in a shallow saucepan.

2. Bring to a boil, turn the heat down, and simmer, uncovered, for 20 to 30 minutes
(possibly longer) until it is reduced by slightly more than half. Remove from heat,
and let it cool.

Apple Chutney
1 1/2kg cooking apples, peeled and diced
750g/26oz light muscovado sugar
500g/18oz raisins
2 medium onions, finely chopped
2 tsps of mustard seeds
2 tsps of ground ginger
1 tsp of salt
700ml/3-1/2 cups cider vinegar

1. Combine all the ingredients in a large, heavy saucepan. Bring the mixture to a boil
over a medium heat, then simmer uncovered, stirring frequently, for 30-40 mins, or
until thick and pulpy. Remove from the heat, leave to cool and transfer to sterilised,
clean, dry jars and seal.

Balsamic Butter
110g/4oz butter, at room temperature
salt and freshly ground black pepper to taste
1 tbsp minced shallots
1 tbsp balsamic vinegar

1. Use a fork to cream all ingredients together. Cover or wrap and refrigerate or
freeze until needed. This gentle butter goes well with baked or sauteed fish dishes,
grilled mild fish, or steamed vegetables.

Herbed Olives and Onion Marinade

450g/16oz olives, rinsed of any brine
2 tbsps red wine vinegar
2 tbsps cane vinegar
110ml/1/2 cup olive oil
110g/4 oz cocktail onions (1 jar)
2 tarragon sprigs
2 parsley sprigs

1. In a large clean glass jar with lid, combine olives, vinegars, olive oil, cocktail onions, tarragon sprigs, parsley sprigs, and salt. Shake well. Marinate at room temperature, shaking jar occasionally, for at least 12 hours.

2. Serve immediately with a little of the marinade and the onions, and the parsley sprigs for garnish, or store marinade for up to 6 months in the refrigerator.

Pickled Relish

900g/32oz courgette/zucchini, sliced thin
2 onions, sliced 1/4 inch thick
4 carrots, 1/4 by 1/4 by 3-inch strips
4 celery sticks, 1/4 by 1/4 by 3-inch strips
12 radishes
2 tbsps salt
675ml/3 cups Red Wine Vinegar
175g/1-1/2 cups sugar
1 tbsp celery seed
1 tbsp fennel seed
2 tbsps ground mustard
3 dried red-hot pepper pods

1. In a large bowl combine courgette, onion, carrot, celery, radishes, and salt. Cover with cold water and let stand 45 minutes. Drain thoroughly. In a large pot combine vinegar, sugar, celery seed, fennel seed, mustard, and pepper pods.

2. Bring to a simmer. Remove from heat and pour over vegetables. Let cool, then refrigerate at least 1 day. To serve, lift vegetables out of their brine with a slotted spoon. Transfer to relish trays or bowls. Vegetables may be stored, in their brine, and refrigerated, for up to 1 month.

Pumpkin Chutney

2.7kg pumpkins, peeled, deseeded and diced

3 oranges

2 lemons

500g/18oz light muscovado sugar

600ml/2-1/2 cups of cider vinegar

1. Place the pumpkin in a bowl and sprinkle liberally with salt. Toss to get it all coated, cover and leave overnight. Drain off any juices, wash in cold water, then drain again to remove excess moisture.

2. Peel and segment the fruit and remove the pith. Tip into a heavy-based pot with all of the remaining ingredients. Bring to the boil over medium heat, then reduce the heat and leave to simmer uncovered, stirring occasionally, for about 40 mins. Cool, then transfer to a sterilised jar and seal.

Spicy blackberry chutney

500g/18oz blackberries

140g/5oz caster sugar

40g/2oz red onions, sliced

3 tbsps chopped fresh root ginger

2 tbspa of Dijon mustard

150ml/2/3 cup white wine vinegar

1. Combine all the ingredients, except the vinegar, in a large saucepan. Stir mixture over medium heat until the blackberries burst. Season with salt and pepper, to taste. Add the vinegar and allow the mixture to simmer uncovered for 10 mins. Cool, transfer to a sterilised jar and seal immediately.

Tomato and Pearl Onion Chutney

1 large onion, minced

2 cloves garlic, minced

1 tbsp olive oil

5 tomatoes, diced

1 tbsp minced fresh ginger

2 tbsps tomato paste

1 tsp dry mustard

2 tbsps pomegranate vinegar

1/2 tsp salt

1 tbsp honey

1/4 tsp ground dried red chillies

50g/1/4 cup raisins

2 tbsps minced parsley

1 tsp fresh oregano, minced

275g/10oz pearl onions, peeled

1. Over a medium heat, saute the onion and garlic in oil for 5 minutes; add tomatoes, ginger, tomato paste, dry mustard, vinegar, salt, honey, dried chiles, raisins, parsley, and oregano. Cook for 20 minutes. Add pearl onions and cook for 25 minutes more. Cool slightly before serving.

Pickled Onions

1.8kg/4 lb pickling onions (unpeeled)

675g/1-1/2 lb salt

2 pints white vinegar

2 tsps salt

2 tsps ground ginger

1 1/2 tsps allspice berries

1 1/2 tsps cloves

6 peppercorns

1. Place the unpeeled onions in a large bowl, sprinkle over the salt and cover with water. Cover the bowl with a plate and set aside for 2 days, stirring occasionally. Drain and peel the onions, return to the bowl, cover with boiling water, set aside for 3 minutes, then drain again.

2. Repeat the process twice more, then pack the onions into hot jars. Place the remaining ingredients in a saucepan and bring slowly to the boil. Reduce the heat and simmer for 15 minutes. Allow to cool slightly, then pour over the onions in the jars making sure they are completely covered.

3. Whilst still hot, cover with a waxed disc (wax side down) then place a cellophane disc over the top then cover with a screw top lid. Cover seal and label with the date then store in a cool dark place for 2-3 months before consuming.

Beetroot, goat's cheese & Tarragon salad

6 raw medium beetroot
2 tbsps white wine vinegar
2 tbsps balsamic vinegar
5 tbsps of olive oil
250g/9oz soft fresh goat's cheese
1 handful fresh tarragon leaves

1. Wash the beetroot and put them in a pan of salted water with the white wine vinegar. Boil for 30-40 minutes or until tender. Drain and leave to cool slightly, then peel - wear a pair of washing up gloves to stop your hands from turning pink.

2. Cut each beetroot into wedges and arrange on a large platter then drizzle the warm beetroot with half the balsamic vinegar and half the olive oil and season with salt and pepper. Break the goat's cheese into pieces over the beetroot and sprinkle on the tarragon and remaining vinegar and oil.

Belgian Endive and Red Pepper Coleslaw with Champagne Vinaigrette

350g/12oz of Belgian endive, cored and cut lengthwise into 1/4" pieces
1 red bell pepper, cored and cut into strips
1 1/2 tbsps Champagne vinegar
3 tbsps olive oil
Salt & freshly ground pepper
Tarragon leaves and pomegranate seeds

1. Toss the endive and the red pepper together. Pour the vinegar and oil into a small screw top jar. Add the salt and pepper and shake vigorously to combine. Pour the dressing over the coleslaw and toss to combine.

2. Divide the coleslaw among 4 plates and top each with a few tarragon leaves and the pomegranate seeds.

Carrots with Tarragon

8 small carrots, sliced 1/4-inch thick
4 tbsps butter
1 tbsp fresh tarragon, chopped

2 tsps balsamic vinegar
1/2 tsp honey
Pinch of sea salt

1. Boil the carrots in salted water until soft, about 10 minutes. Drain the carrots. Melt the butter in a saucepan, add the rest of the ingredients and stir together. Toss the carrots in the flavoured butter and serve hot.

Chicken with Tarragon Vinegar

1 chicken, cut into 8 serving pieces, rinsed and dried
3 tbsps olive oil
3 tbsps unsalted butter
110ml/1/2 cup dry white wine
4 shallots, minced
2 medium tomatoes, peeled, seeded and chopped
110m/1/2 cup white wine tarragon vinegar
1 bunch tarragon leaves, minced

1. In a deep sided skillet or pan, heat the oil with 1 Tablespoon of the butter over high heat. Season the chicken with salt and pepper and cook the chicken about 12 minutes on each side. Watch the heat so that the skin does not scorch.

2. The cooking can be done in batches if the skillet is not large enough to hold the chicken in a single layer. Remove the chicken and cover with aluminum foil to keep warm. Pour off fat.

3. Return skillet to medium heat and deglaze with the white wine. Add the shallots and tomatoes. Cook for several minutes then raise the heat to high and slowly add the vinegar. Cook for 2-3 minutes.

4. Whisk in the remaining 2 tbsps of the butter. Cook for 1 more minute. Return chicken to skillet, coat well with sauce. Cover and cook about 3 more minutes. Sprinkle with the tarragon. Serve, accompanied by sautéed potatoes.

Chicken Skewers with Cucumber Dip

500g/18oz boneless, skinless chicken breasts
4 tbsps chopped coriander
1 tsp coarsely ground black peppercorns
2 limes, juice only
1 tsp light muscovado sugar
2 garlic cloves, crushed
1 tbsp of vegetable oil

Dip Ingredients:
110ml/1 cup rice vinegar
2 tbsps of sugar
1 red chilli, deseeded and finely chopped
1 shallot, thinly sliced
1 cucumber

1. Cut the chicken into thin slices. Mix the coriander, pepper, lime juice, sugar, garlic and oil. Toss the chicken in this mixture, then thread onto 12 bamboo skewers. You can make these up to a day ahead and chill until ready to cook.

2. To make the dip, heat the vinegar and sugar in a small pan until the sugar has dissolved, then increase the heat and boil for 3 minutes, until slightly syrupy. Remove from the heat and stir in the chilli and shallot. Leave to cool.

3. Thinly slice a 5cm piece of cucumber, quarter each slice and add to the dip. Cut the rest of the cucumber into thin sticks. Cook the chicken under a preheated grill for 3-4 minutes each side, then serve with the dipping sauce, cucumber sticks, rice and pak choi.

Cucumber Sambal

1 cucumber
1 tsp minced onion
1 tsp minced green pepper
1 tsp chopped parsley
1 tbsp vinegar mixed with a pinch of sugar
1 tsp olive oil

1. Peel the cucumber. Cut it into thin strips about 1-inch long. Mix the onion, green pepper and parsley together. Whisk the vinegar and olive oil together and pour over the cucumbers.

Pasta with Balsamic Tomatoes and Mozzarella

400g/14oz pasta
250g/9oz cherry tomatoes, quartered
30ml/2 Tablespoons of olive oil
30ml/2 Tablespoons of balsamic vinegar
2 x 125g balls of mozzarella, cubed
bunch of basil, leaves roughly torn
grated parmesan, to serve

1. Cook the pasta following pack instructions. Drain, reserving a few tablespoons of water in the pan. Return pasta to the pan over a medium heat and add the tomatoes, oil and balsamic vinegar.

2. Cook for 1-2 minutes, then season and stir through mozzarella and basil. Serve with grated parmesan.

Peaches with Prosciutto and Blue Cheese

4 ripe peaches, stoned and quartered
4 tbsps of olive oil
100g/4oz bag of rocket
100g/4oz blue cheese, crumbled
85g/3oz pack prosciutto
1 tbsp of balsamic vinegar

1. Brush the peach quarters with 2 tablespoons of the olive oil and grind a little black pepper over. Heat a griddle pan until really hot, add the peaches, cooking for 2-3 minutes on each cut side until caramelised. Set aside.

2. Toss the rocket in 1 tablespoon of the olive oil and pile up with the cheese and prosciutto on 4 plates. Top with the peach quarters. Whisk together the remaining oil and the vinegar, spoon over the salad and serve.

Pork Chops Balsamic

4 thick, boneless loin pork chops
herb seasoning mix
110ml/1/2 cup balsamic vinegar
75ml/1/3 cup chicken broth
cooking spray
salt and pepper

1. Spray a nonstick skillet with the cooking spray and heat over med-high heat. Sprinkle both sides of the chops with seasoning and add to the skillet.

2. Sear 1 minute on each side, then reduce heat to medium. Cook 4-6 minutes on each side. Remove from skillet and keep warm. Lightly wipe the skillet with a paper towel. Return to heat and add vinegar and broth.

3. Cook for 5-6 minutes, stirring occasionally. Spoon the sauce over the pork chops. Serve with couscous and roasted asparagus.

Warm Potato Salad with Tomatoes, Celery and Chives

1kg/2-1/4 lbs. potatoes, quartered
175g/1/2 cup mayonnaise
15ml/1 tbsp olive oil
10ml/2 tsps cider vinegar
1 garlic clove, pressed through a garlic press
1/4 cup finely chopped fresh chives
4 celery sticks thinly sliced on the diagonal
525g/1-1/2 cups grape or cherry tomatoes, halved

1. Cover the potatoes with salted cold water and simmer until tender - about 20 minutes. Whisk together the mayonnaise, oil, vinegar, garlic, chives and season with salt and pepper.

2. Drain the potatoes in a colander and cool for 5 minutes. Add the potatoes to the dressing, toss briefly. Add the tomatoes and celery and toss again. Season with salt and pepper.

Slow Roasted Salmon with a horseradish vinaigrette

4 x 200g/7-oz. salmon fillets
olive oil for brushing the fish
sea salt & freshly ground black pepper
1-1/2 tbsps salted capers, rinsed
75g/3 oz. baby spinach leaves
50g/2 oz. curly endive
25g/1 oz lambs lettuce

For the dressing:
1 tbsp red wine vinegar
1/2 cup extra-virgin olive oil
1 tbsp horseradish

1. Preheat oven to 175°F/325°C/Gas Mark 3. Lightly oil a baking tray. Brush the salmon with oil and sprinkle with salt and pepper. Place the fillets on the oiled baking tray and sprinkle the capers over the fish. Place in the oven and bake for about 15 minutes or until the salmon is firm to the touch. Remove from oven and set aside for 5 minutes.

2. In the meantime, make the dressing. Whisk the vinegar, oil and horseradish together. Toss the mixed greens with the dressing. Divide the mixed greens among 4 serving plates, top with the salmon and scatter the capers over.

Spiced Cherries

450g/1 lb. cherries
565ml/2-1/2 cups white vinegar
grated rind of 1 lemon
150g/1-1/4 cups packed brown sugar
3 whole cloves
2 cinnamon sticks, broken into 1 inch pieces

1. Wash the cherries and allow to dry overnight. Trim stems to 1/2-inch. Put the vinegar, lemon rind, brown sugar, cloves and cinnamon into a saucepan. Bring to a boil, reduce heat and allow to simmer until all of the sugar is dissolved.

2. Remove from heat and allow to cool. Put the cherries into jars and pour the cooled vinegar mixture over them. Place in a cool, dark place, 2 weeks before using.

Strawberries with Balsamic Vinegar and Vodka

12 medium-sized strawberries
4 tsps of Balsamic Vinegar
4 tsps of sugar
4 measures of Vodka

1. Chop the medium-sized strawberries and place into 4 bowls. Add 1 tsp of Balsamic Vinegar and 1 tsp of sugar and 1 measure of Vodka to each bowl. Serve with mint leaf for garnish.

Tomatoes, Greek style with white wine vinegar, lemon juice and spices

900g/2 lbs. small tomatoes, quartered
55ml/1/4 cup olive oil
1 garlic clove, pressed
55ml/1/4 cup white wine vinegar
15ml/1 tbsp freshly squeezed lemon juice
1/2 tsp ground coriander
2 cucumbers, cut half lengthwise, seeds scooped out, then sliced into 1/2-inch slices
1 tbsp minced, fresh oregano

1. Season the quartered tomatoes with salt and freshly ground pepper. Heat the olive oil over medium heat. Add the garlic, vinegar, lemon juice and coriander. Simmer for 1 minute then pour the hot vinaigrette over the tomatoes and allow to marinate at room temperature until cool.

2. Just before serving, sprinkle the tomatoes with the oregano. Season the cucumber with salt and pepper and put them in a separate bowl.

Trout with Tomato Vinaigrette

4 freshwater trout fillets (about 225g/8 oz. each)
450ml/2 cups vegetable broth
110ml/1/2 cup red wine vinegar
salt & freshly ground pepper

1. In a large casserole, combine the vegetable stock and the vinegar and bring to a boil. Sprinkle the trout fillets with salt and pepper. When the stock is boiling, add the fillets, return stock to a boil, and cook for 1 minute.

2. Using a slotted spoon, remove the trout and place on a serving platter. Spoon the vinaigrette (page 49) across the middle of the fish and serve.

Tuna with Balsamic Vinegar Glaze

2 1/2 tsps black pepper, freshly ground
1/2 tsp salt
8 tuna steaks (175g/6oz each), 3/4 inch thick
110ml/1/2 cup chicken stock
20ml/ 2 tbsps balsamic vinegar
1 tbsp dark brown sugar
2 tsps soy sauce
1 tsp cornflour
2 spring onions, sliced diagonally

1. Prepare a grill pan or barbecue grill to medium heat and spray with cooking oil or brush lightly. Sprinkle the fish with salt and pepper and place on the grill. Cook each tuna steak for 3 minutes on each side and then remove from heat.

2. While the fish is cooking, combine all of the remaining ingredients in a saucepan. Cook for two minutes on medium heat, stirring constantly. Spoon glaze over fish before serving.

Winter Salad

1 butternut squash, cut into thin wedges
2 red onions, halved and cut into wedges
4 parsnips, cut into wedges
3 tbsps of olive oil
1-2 tbsps of clear honey
1 ciabatta, roughly torn into pieces
225g leaf spinach
2 tbsps of white wine vinegar
1 tsp Dijon mustard

1. Heat oven to 220C/450F/Gas Mark 7. Put the vegetables into a large roasting tin, drizzle with half the oil and season to taste. Roast for 20 minutes, turning once in a while until softened. Drizzle with the honey. Scatter the torn toasted ciabatta over the top and return to the oven for a further 5 mins or until toasted.

Winter Salad/cont.

2. Put the spinach into a large bowl and tip in the vegetables and ciabatta. Whisk the vinegar, mustard and remaining oil together, season to taste and toss into the salad until the spinach wilts slightly. Serve immediately.

Winter Vegetables with Lancashire cheese

1 large butternut squash
1 medium red onion
6 tbsps of olive oil
1 large sprig fresh sage
1 large courgette/zucchini
1 tbsp of balsamic or sherry vinegar
100g Lancashire cheese

1. Preheat the oven to fan 180C/350F/Gas Mark 4. Using a sharp knife, cut the squash in half and scoop out the seeds. Cut the halves into smaller pieces so you can peel them more easily. Chop the flesh into big bite-sized pieces - they don't have to be neat.

2. Halve the onion and trim the root end leaving a little on to hold the segments together. Peel and then cut each half into four wedges. Scatter the squash and onion in a large roasting tin so they have plenty of room to roast, drizzle over 5 tbsps of the oil and toss together.

3. Strip the sage leaves from the stem and roughly chop - you should have about 2 tbsps. Scatter over the vegetables and season. Roast for 20 minutes, stirring once halfway through.

4. Meanwhile, slice the courgette thickly and toss with the remaining oil. Remove the roasting tin from the oven and push the partly cooked squash and onion to the side. Put the courgette slices flat on the base and season. Roast for a further 10 minutes, until all the vegetables are tender.

5. Remove tin from the oven, sprinkle the vinegar over the vegetables and toss. Crumble over the Lancashire cheese. Toss lightly so the cheese melts a little and serve.

Health and Beauty

Apple cider vinegar has been used since around 3000 B.C. because of it's powerful healing and remedial qualities. The health benefits that come along with using apple cider vinegar as a healing agent are plentiful. It benefits not only men, women and children, but can be of great benefit to the health of animals. It is a powerful elixir and naturally occurring antibiotic.

A wonderful benefit of apple cider vinegar is that it is extremely helpful to people with arthritis. It breaks down calcium deposits while re-mineralizing bones. Some external benefits of apple cider vinegar include the soothing of irritated skin, the relief of muscle pain from exercise, maintaining healthy skin and promotes youthful, healthy bodies.

Apple cider vinegar is a purifier and is extremely effective in detoxicating many organs in conjunction with the blood stream. It is also very effective at breaking down various deposits within the human body, and therefore promotes the health of organs such as the bladder, kidneys and liver, by helping to prevent excessive alkaline in the urine. It also helps to keep blood thin so that it does not become too thick and amplify the possibility of a strained heart, resulting in high blood pressure. Apple cider vinegar can also be used to promote proper digestion and can help neutralize toxic substances that are taken into the body during food consumption.

Potassium, found abundantly in apple cider vinegar, is essential in normal body growth and function. Sinus troubles, excessive mucus, tooth decay, unhealthy fingernails, and watery eyes are all signs of deficient potassium levels in the body and can be remedied by ingesting apple cider vinegar. It can even be taken to prevent hair loss, as lowered potassium levels can cause failure of the body to reproduce worn-out tissues. Potassium also acts as a restraint for those who suffer from nervousness or hyper-activeness. One of the most widely known and greatest benefits of apple cider vinegar is that it promotes good digestion and can help keep you at a healthy weight. It contains Apple Pectin, a dietary fibre that is an essential part of a healthy diet. Containing over 90 substances and endless vitamins and minerals, the benefits of apple cider vinegar as a part of your daily diet are impossible to ignore.

Age spots

Mix equal parts of onion juice and apply cider vinegar and use it daily on age spots. You should notice a difference within a couple of weeks.

Arthritis

If you suffer from arthritis, remedy the pain by placing 2 teaspoons of apple cider vinegar and honey in a glass of water and stirring vigorously. Drink several times daily.

Arthritis - pain relief

Localize treatment for arthritic pain by soaking hand or foot joints in a solution of warm water and apple cider vinegar two or three times a day. Knees and shoulder joints can be treated by placing a poultice made from soaking a cloth in the same solution, then wrapping around the afflicted area. Secure with a plastic wrap (cling-film/cellowrap) and cover with a towel. Once the cloth cools, repeat the process.

Athlete's Foot

Before going to bed, soak your feet in vinegar for several minutes. Although it may sting at first, it isn't severe and the discomfort will pass quickly. Afterwards, soak a sock in a mixture of two parts water and one part vinegar and place it on your foot. Keep it on for 30 minutes, then remove and pat your foot dry. Repeat the process the next morning and continue until the infection is gone.

Asthma

In addition to, rather than as a substitute for, any prescription from your medical professional, mix 1 tablespoon of apple cider vinegar with a glass of water and sip regularly over the course of half an hour. Wheezing should lessen and breathing become easier.

Boils

One tablespoon of apple cider vinegar and one tablespoon of honey mixed with hot water and drank twice a day can bring relief from painful boils.

Bones

Apple cider contains manganese, magnesium, silicon and calcium which are all proven to sustain bone mass, something crucial in the fight against osteoporosis. Look for apple cider supplements to take regularly, particularly if you have a calcium deficiency or are entering post-menopause where there is a risk of loss of bone density.

Bruises and swelling

Mix a solution of equal parts apple cider vinegar and cold water. Soak a clean cloth or rag in the solution, then wring out and wrap it around the area which is bruised or swollen. Hold the compress in place with a bandage and leave for at least an hour, longer if possible, as the longer you leave this the better the results.

Cholesterol

To help reduce cholesterol levels, try drinking half a cup of this solution before you eat the largest meal of the day. 450ml/2 cups of grape juice, 225ml/1 cup of apple juice and 55ml/1/4 cup of white distilled vinegar. Combine all of the ingredients together and chill before drinking.

Cold Sore

Dry up a cold sore by dabbing it with a cotton ball saturated in white distilled vinegar three times a day. The vinegar will quickly soothe the pain and swelling.

Constipation

Pectin, found in apple cider vinegar, can assist your body with regular bowel movements. Try a daily dose of 5ml/1 teaspoon to aid digestive acids and so relieve constipation.

Corn and callus remover

Soak a piece of stale bread (a cloth would probably do as well) in apple cider vinegar, and tape it over the callus or corn overnight.

Cough

Combine 10ml/2 teaspoons of apple cider vinegar with 10ml/2 teaspoons of honey in a glass of water and sip regularly throughout the day.

Cough - persistent

Combine 15ml/1 tablespoon of apple cider vinegar with 1 tablespoon of butter and 1 tablespoon of sugar. Melt together in a small pan and then take whilst still warm.

Cuts and abrasions

Clean minor cuts and abrasions with a solution made from equal parts apple cider vinegar and water.

Dentures

Leave your dentures in apple cider vinegar for as long as you would leave them in a denture cleanser - about 15 minutes to half an hour, or longer, if you wish. Then brush them thoroughly.

Deodorant

Wipe your underarms with white distilled vinegar which is a natural deodorant. This will not stop perspiration but will neutralize odour.

Diabetes

Added dietary fibre, such as contained in apple cider vinegar, is beneficial in controlling blood glucose levels.

Diarrhoea

One teaspoon of apple cider vinegar diluted in a glass of water, taken 6 times daily when suffering from a bought of diarrhoea can lessen the intensity and allow the natural course of elimination to take place.

Digestion

If you take one teaspoon of apple cider vinegar with or just before a meal, this isolates the fat in food and it passes through your system and aids digestion. Apple cider vinegar contains acetic acid which stimulates the production of stomach acid. The more stomach acid the better as it breaks down your food into smaller molecules. The smaller the molecules the more efficiently your intestines and liver can absorb the nutrients it needs.

Earwash - waxy build-up

An effective way to remove wax from the ear is to combine equal parts of white distilled vinegar and warm water and gently rinse the ear. Do not use cold water or cotton wool/earbuds.

Eyeglasses

Applying a few drops of white vinegar to your glass lenses and wiping them with a soft cloth will easily remove dirt, sweat, and fingerprints, and leave them spotless. Don't use vinegar on plastic lenses, however.

Eyes

Taking two teaspoons each of apple cider vinegar and honey dissolved in water 3 times a day can stop the onset of tiredness and supply the body with vital elements essential to the health of your eyes.

Fatigue

Apple cider vinegar in drinking water is very effective in eliminating the low-grade fevers that are present in Chronic Fatigue sufferers. It also helps eliminate the 'thrush' coating in the mouth which is sometimes caused by antibiotic use. Mix four tablespoons of apple cider vinegar to a litre of drinking water. Drink up to one litre each day.

Foot - odour

Bathing your feet in 1 part apple cider vinegar and 1 part warm water will remove foot odour.

Free radicals

Beta-carotene, found in apple cider vinegar, is an extremely powerful natural antioxidant and can help neutralise the free radicals formed in our body.

Gallstones and Kidney Stones

It is alleged that the acids found in apple cider vinegar are beneficial in breaking down gallstones and kidney stones.

Haemorrhoids

Soothe the itching and burning of hemorrhoids by taking a cotton ball and dabbing the affected area with full strength apple cider vinegar. If you find the full strength solution stings, dilute the vinegar half and half with water.

Hair - chlorine

Unfortunately, if you have fair hair and swim regularly, you may find your hair taking on a green hue. Keep this from happening by rubbing 55ml/1/4 cup of apple cider vinegar into your hair and letting it set for 15 minutes before swimming.

Hair - colour preserver

To prevent your new hair colour fading, rinse with a solution of 1 part white distilled vinegar to 2 parts cold water (as cold as you can stand). This will seal the colour and prevent fading.

Hair - conditioner, intensive

Combinine 1 teaspoon of apple cider vinegar with 2 tablespoons olive oil and 3 egg whites. Rub the mixture into your hair, then keep it covered for 30 minutes using plastic wrap or a shower cap. After this time, shampoo hair as normal.

Hair - dandruff

To give your dandruff the brush-off, follow up each shampoo by rinsing in a solution made of equal parts apple cider vinegar and water. You can also fight dandruff by applying 3 tablespoons vinegar onto your hair and massaging into your scalp before you shampoo. Wait a few minutes, then rinse it out and wash as usual.

Hair - frizz reduction

To eliminate the frizz from over processed hair, rinse your hair with four parts water and one part apple cider vinegar after every shampoo.

Hair - lice

It is also helpful when children get lice, if you take warm apple cider vinegar and apply to their hair (perhaps as a final rinse when washing their hair). Also dip your nit comb in the vinegar and as you run it through the hair it helps remove the nits. It is alleged to be able to help break down the glue the nits use to stay attached to the hair.

Hair - promote growth

Hair loss is often caused by a tissue salt deficiency, but drinking a daily solution of one teaspoon of apple cider vinegar in a glass of water can re-establish a natural balance and supply deficiencies. This is a long-term treatment and it could take a couple of months to take effect.

Hair - rinse

Used as a hair rinse, vinegar neutralizes the alkali left by shampoos and gives hair extra shine.

Hands - conditioning spray

Spray your hands with a mist of apple cider vinegar, or dip them in vinegar and dry after washing dishes or having them in soapy water, to keep your hands soft.

Hangover cures

Soak a cloth with apple cider vinegar and place on your forehead to stop hangover headaches.

Hay-Fever

As an effective relief from the onslaught of hay-fever, prepare your body to fight back by taking a tablespoon of honey after each meal roughly 2 weeks prior to the beginning of the hay-fever season, and then drink a mixture of 2 tablespoons of apple cider vinegar and 2 tablespoons of honey disolved in a glass of water 3 times daily for the duration of the hay-fever season.

Heartburn

If you suffer from heartburn, drink 1 teaspoon of apple cider vinegar in a glass of water prior to eating.

Hiccups

Drinking one teaspoon of apple cider vinegar gets rid of hiccups.

High Blood Pressure

Two teaspoons of apple cider vinegar and two teaspoons of honey in a glass of water, drunk 3-4 times daily helps maintain the balance between proteins and carbohydrates which is essential if you suffer from high blood pressure.

Hot Flushes

Take 1 or 2 teaspoons of apple cider vinegar with a glass of water 3 times a day or more and the hot flushes should go right away. The taste is not bad at all and it doesn't upset your stomach.

Insect bites and stings

Soak a cotton ball in cider vinegar and hold to the sore spot, or tape it on with bandage tape. Within a few minutes the pain stops. This works very well on wasp stings, but if you are going to try this on bee stings, ensure that you remove the stinger first.

Insect bites and stings - remedy 2

Make a thick paste of cornflour and apple cider vinegar and apply it to the itchy, irritated area. As it dries, the paste pulls the poison out of the skin, relieving the pain and preventing swelling.

Insomnia

If you are suffering from lack of sleep, mix 15ml of apple cider vinegar with 275ml of honey and take 2 teaspoons of the mixture before going to bed. If after an hour you are still wide awake, repeat the dosage.

Irritable bowel syndrome

Relieve the symptoms of irritable bowel syndrome by sipping a glass of water mixed with a teaspoon of apple cider vinegar.

Jellyfish sting

If you are stung by a jellyfish, pouring some undiluted vinegar on the sting will take away the pain in no time, and let you scrape out the stinger with a plastic credit card. However, using vinegar on stings inflicted by the jellyfish's cousin, the Portuguese man-of-war, is now discouraged because vinegar may actually increase the amount of toxin released under the skin. Warning: If you have difficulty breathing or the sting area becomes inflamed and swollen, get medical attention at once; you could be having an allergic reaction.

Kidneys and Bladder

From time to time we can benefit from "flushing" through the kidneys and bladder. Two teaspoons of apple cider vinegar in a glass of water 6 times a day will act as a cleaning agent for these organs.

Manicure - cuticles

You can soften the cuticles on your fingers and toes before manicuring them by soaking your digits in a bowl of undiluted white distilled vinegar for five minutes.

Manicure - nail polish

Nail polish will go on smoother, and stay longer if you clean your finger nails with white distilled vinegar before applying nail polish.

Menopause

If you are taking calcium-magnesium supplements, wash these down by drinking a glass of water with 2 teaspoons of apple cider vinegar as this will dissolve the calcium and allow it to be more easily absorbed in the body.

Mouthwash - bad breath

After eating garlic or onions, a quick and easy way to sweeten your breath is to rinse your mouth with a solution made by dissolving 2 tablespoons apple cider vinegar and 1 teaspoon salt in a glass of warm water.

Muscle compress

For those very painful "Charlie Horses" and muscle cramps, mix a solution of half vinegar and half water, onto a small towel or flannel. Heat in the microwave for 20 seconds and place on the pained area.

Muscle cramps

Quite often caused by too low a level of potassium, take 1 teaspoon of apple cider vinegar on the onset of cramp to relieve the condition.

Muscle relaxant

Add 2 cups of apple cider vinegar to the warm water in your bathtub to soak sore muscles and soothe away aches and pains.

Muscle - sprain

Mix apple cider vinegar with red clay, heat it and make a paste. Place on the sprain and then wrap with strips of an old sheet. After an hour, soak the paste off with warm water and the sprain should feel a lot better.

Nail Fungus

Both white vinegar and apple cider vinegar are effective in the eradication of fungal infections from toenails or fingernails. The most common method is daily foot baths in a solution made from equal parts vinegar and water. Alternate between warm and cold baths, ensuring that you soak your feet for at least 30 minutes. For the successful treatment of fungal infections, it is recommend that you have 3 baths a day, morning, noon and evening. You can also apply 2 drops of vinegar directly on the base of the nail twice a day. However, you must make sure that vinegar will remain in place long enough to benefit from its action.

Nails - brittle

Strengthen brittle and weak nails by soaking for 5 minutes in full-strength apple cider vinegar.

Nasal Congestion

Add 55ml/1/4 cup white distilled vinegar to the water in your hot-steam vaporizer (or a bowl of boiling water) to help ease congestion caused by a chest cold or sinus infection. Note: Check with the manufacturer before adding vinegar to a cool-mist vaporizer.

Nausea

Sip on one teaspoon in a half to three-quarters cup of water. Honey may be added if desired to enhance flavour.

Nose bleeds

If you suffer from a nose bleed, drinking two teaspoons of vinegar in water 3 times daily can restore the natural clotting properties of blood.

Pedicure

Put 110ml/1/2 cup of apple cider vinegar into a large bowl to soak your feet in before a pedicure as this will soften your skin.

Piercing - infections

As vinegar is a natural antiseptic, bathing the infected piercing in apple cider vinegar can relieve the symptoms.

Skin - acne

To get rid of unsightly blemishes, mix one part apple cider vinegar with 10 parts water and put in a clean glass bottle. After washing your face as usual, dab the solution on your spots with a cotton ball. You can do this several times a day without drying out your skin. Vinegar helps adjust the pH balance in your skin, thereby treating and preventing new breakouts.

Skin - blackheads and blocked pores

Mash three large strawberries and mix them with 55ml/1/4 cup of apple cider vinegar. Let the mixture stand for two hours, then strain it through a cheesecloth. Apply to your face and leave it on overnight. Wash your face with cool water and a mild soap in the morning.

Skin - cracked or chapped

Heal cracked, chapped skin by gently applying a mixture of half apple cider vinegar and half water.

Skin - dry and itchy skin

A few drops of apple cider vinegar in the bathwater can soothe skin.

Skin - minor burns

Splash some white distilled vinegar on a bit of paper towel and put it on the burn. It stops hurting immediately and if you keep it on, you will not develop a blister.

Skin - psoriasis

If you suffer with this condition, mix a solution of 3 parts apple cider vinegar and 1 part water into a spray bottle. Shower as usual and then spritz your body with the vinegar solution. Rinse solution off your skin and soft pat skin dry. The vinegar will ensure that there is no soap residue left on your skin and reduce itchiness.

Skin - rashes

Rashes caused by exposure to poison ivy or poison oak can be eased by gently dabbing the area with a cotton ball or soft cloth saturated with white or cider vinegar.

Skin - sunburn remedy

At bedtime, cover sunburns with a towel soaked in an equal part mix of apple cider vinegar and water and try to persuade the victim to sleep this way.

Skin - sunburn remedy, spray

Put apple cider vinegar in a spray bottle and spray on sunburn and this will soothe the effected area.

Skin - swelling due to sun exposure

To relieve swelling and fluid from too much sun, mix a paste of baking soda and apple cider vinegar and apply to the effected area.

Skin - toner

After you wash your face, mix 1 tablespoon of apple cider vinegar with 2 cups of water as a finishing rinse to cleanse and tighten your skin. You can also make your own facial treatment by mixing 1/4 cup apple cider vinegar with 1/4 cup water. Gently apply the solution to your face and let it dry.

Stiff neck

Mix a solution of equal parts apple cider vinegar and warm water. Soak a clean cloth in the solution, then wring out and wrap it around your neck. Hold the rag in place by wrapping loosely with cling-film/cellowrap and then cover with a towel. Take extra care to ensure that whilst the wrap is comfortable it is not too tight, i.e beware of strangulation. Leave this on over night.

Tendonitis

To ease the pain, soak the effected area in warm apple cider vinegar until the pain subsides.

Throat - sore throat, remedy 1

Mix 1 tablespoon of apple cider vinegar in a glass of warm water for a sore throat. Gargle every hour and swallow after gargling, with two mouthfuls. If started at the first hint of a sore throat, this remedy usually works.

Throat - sore throat, remedy 2

If your throat is left raw by a bad cough, or even a speaking or singing engagement, you'll find fast relief by gargling with 1 tablespoon apple cider vinegar and 1 teaspoon salt dissolved in a glass of warm water; use several times a day if needed.

Throat - sore throat, remedy 3

For sore throats associated with a cold or flu, combine 55ml/1/4 cup of apple cider vinegar and 55ml/1/4 cup honey and take 1 tablespoon every four hours.

Throat - sore throat, remedy 4

To soothe both a cough and a sore throat, mix 110ml/1/2 cup apple cider vinegar, 110ml/1/2 cup water, 20ml/4 teaspoons honey, and 1 teaspoon worcester sauce. Swallow 1 tablespoon four or five times daily, including one before bedtime. Warning: Children under one year old should never be given honey.

Throat - tickly throat

To create a homemade throat soother, take equal amounts of honey and cider vinegar, stir or shake until dissolved. Take a tablespoon at a time to cut mucus in the throat.

Tooth - ache

Soak a cotton in apple cider vinegar, place it on the aching tooth and bite down - in moments the toothache is temporarily gone, giving you time to get to a dentist.

Tooth - whitening

Dipping a wet toothbrush in white distilled vinegar and brushing your teeth will help maintain the colour of your teeth, if not improve the whiteness. This treatment should only be undertaken once a week, and it is essential to rinse thoroughly with clean water as over a prolonged period the vinegar will begin to desolve the calcium and enamel of your teeth.

Vaginal irritation/yeast infections

A few tablespoons of apple cider vinegar in the bathwater can help vaginal irritation (vaginitis). Bathe regularly until symptoms disappear.

Varicose veins

Splash apple cider vinegar on your varicose veins. The vinegar will reduce the veins and relieve the pain and swelling.

Warts

Put apple cider vinegar on a plaster and wrap it over the wart, replace the plaster each night and after about a week the wart should have gone.

Weight loss

It's an ongoing battle as to whether vinegar can help you lose weight, but the ones who say it will, say to drink a glass of water before each meal in which you've added a tablespoon of apple cider vinegar and a tablespoon of honey.

Pet Care

Bird Cage
Mix a solution of 1 part white distilled vinegar to 2 parts water and use to clean your bird cage and ornaments. It is particularly effective on the removal of bird droppings. After wiping with the vinegar solution, wipe again with clean water.

Brush
Clean your pet's brush and comb by dipping in apple cider vinegar and then rinsing with cold water. This will stop bacteria forming.

Cat Litter tray odour
When you have washed the litter tray, rinse it out and pour about 1/2 inch of full-strength white distilled vinegar into the tray. Let it stand for 20 minutes or so, then swish it around, rinse with cold water, and dry the box. The acid in the vinegar neutralizes the ammonia smell.

Cat Urine Odours
If kitty has had an accident on washable material, mix 110-225ml/1/2 - 1 cup of white distilled vinegar to your laundry, and wash as normal.

Chickens
Add vinegar to chicken's water, especially in the winter, to keep them laying better and stay healthy. If your chickens don't have access to wild, natural food, give it to them year round.

Coat conditioner - cat or dog
Add a teaspoon of apple cider vinegar to your cat or dog's drinking water which will provide additional nutrients to its diet, giving it a shinier and healthier-looking coat.

Dog Blanket
For damp doggy smells, when you next wash the dog blanket add 110ml/1/2 cup white distilled water to the final rinse cycle.

Dog Toys

Clean and disinfect your dog toys regularly with this natural antibiotic. Soak the toys in apple cider vinegar for 10-15 minutes and then rinse in cold water. Allow to dry naturally.

Ear Cleaning

Mix 1/3 rubbing alcohol and 1/3 white distilled vinegar and 1/3 water to create an ear cleaning solution for your cat or dog. Using a dropper, squirt 8-10 drops in ear holding head to side; let it stand in the ear for a minute then drain. While holding their head tilted, massage the ear around in a circle then tilt and wipe out with tissue. Apply once a month or if your animal is scratching. However, if after cleaning the scratching persists they have mites or a bacterial infection and you should take them to the vet.

Eliminate brown patches on your lawn

If you add a teaspoon of apple cider vinegar to your dog's drinking water this will neutralize the acid in the urine and prevent brown patches occurring.

Fish

Use white vinegar to clean the mineral deposits that accumulate at the top of your fish aquarium. Take a hand towel and soak it in the white vinegar. Then, simply wipe around the inside of the tank where the water has evaporated and left the white mineral deposits. You can also use it to clean aquarium ornaments. It is harmless to my fish so I don't worry if some of the vinegar happens to get into the water.

Flea and tick deterrent

Add a teaspoon of apple cider vinegar to your dog or cat's drinking water which will act as a natural deterrent to fleas and ticks.

Flea and Tick repellant

Directly protect your dog against fleas and ticks - fill a spray bottle with equal parts water and apple cider vinegar and apply it directly to the dog's coat and rub it in well. This is safe to use on puppies too.

Hamster Cage

Mix a solution of 1 part white distilled vinegar to 2 parts water and use to clean your hamster cage and wheel. After wiping with the vinegar solution, wipe again with clean water.

Hip dysplasia

Apple cider vinegar breaks down calcium deposits while re-mineralizing bones, and can be used for dogs who suffer from hip dysplasia. Put a teaspoon in with their drinking water daily.

Horse coat conditioner

Mix a solution of 110ml/1/2 cup apple cider vinegar to a litre of water and spray onto the coat of a horse which works like a vinegar hair rinse. Their coat will gleam and it is an economical alternative to expensive show shine products.

Horse Flies

Put 55ml/1/4 cup of apple cider vinegar in with your horse's feed and this will reduce the number of bites from horse flies.

Horse joints

For reducing swelling on a horse (or any animal), wrap the leg in a rag soaked in apple cider vinegar. Wrap in plastic and then bandage to hold it in place - leave on for 4 or more hours.

Housetraining - floor

When housetraining a puppy or kitten, it will often wet previously soiled spots. After cleaning up the mess, it is essential to remove the scent from your floor, carpeting, or sofa. And nothing does that better than vinegar. Blot up as much of the stain as possible. Then mop with equal parts white distilled vinegar and warm water. On a wood or vinyl floor, test a few drops of vinegar in an inconspicuous area to make sure it won't harm the finish. Dry with a cloth or paper towel.

Housetraining - upholstery

For carpets, rugs, and upholstery, thoroughly blot the area with a towel or some rags. Then pour a bit of undiluted white distilled vinegar over the spot. Blot it up with a towel, then reapply the vinegar and let it air-dry. Once the vinegar dries, the spot should be completely deodorized and stop your pet "reoffending"!

Odour removal

If your dog has decided to have a roll in something particularly nasty - add vinegar to their bath water to get rid of the smell.

Puppy Training

Put 1 teaspoon of white distilled vinegar into a spray gun of water to teach your puppy to behave.

Rabbit Hutch

Mix a solution of 1 part white distilled vinegar to 2 parts warm water and use to clean your rabbit hutch to elimate odours. After wiping with the vinegar solution, wipe again with clean water

Rabbit Tray

Rid your house of nasty rabbit odours by rinsing the tray with white distilled vinegar and cold water when cleaning.

Skincare

If your dog suffers from skin infections, after their weekly bath, rinse them with a solution of 1 part apple cider vinegar to 3 parts water.

Water Bowl

If you keep a water bowl in the garden for your pets, wash regularly with a solution of 1 part white distilled vinegar and 1 part water and then rinse with clean cold water. This will remove any mildew.

Malt

As explained in the introduction, malt vinegar is made by malting barley, causing the starch in the grain to turn to maltose. An ale is then brewed from the maltose and allowed to turn into vinegar, which is then aged. It is typically light brown in colour.

Specifically it is used for:

Absorbs excess fat
Cleaning glass
Cleaning coffee pots
Detergent
Disinfectant
Fish and Chips
Flavouring beer
Flavour enhancer for:
Peppercorns
Allspice
Cloves
Chillies
Cabbage
Watery vegetables

Making picalilli
Pickling Onions
Pickling Walnuts

Apple cider

Apple cider vinegar, sometimes known simply as cider vinegar, is made from cider or apple must.

Specifically it is used for:

Base for herb vinegar
Beauty treatments
Fruit salads
Hair care
Medicinal qualities and uses

Wine

Wine vinegar is made from red or white wine, champagne, sherry, or pinot grigio.

Specifically it is used for:

Basting
Bernaise sauce
Fruit salads
Flavoured with:-
Herbs
Honey
Spices

Hollandaise sauce

Marinade
Replacement for cream/butter
Salad dressings
Salsas
Soups
Stews
Vinaigrettes

Fruit

Fruit vinegars are made from fruit wines without any additional flavouring. Common flavours of fruit vinegar include blackcurrant, raspberry, quince, and tomato.

Specifically it is used for:

Cooking duck
Cooking ham
Fruit salads
Pineapple vinegar as a substitute for apple cider vinegar

White

White vinegar, made by oxidizing a distilled alcohol is used for culinary as well as cleaning purposes.

Specifically it is used for:

Beauty treatments
Cleaning solutions
Combined with:-
Basil
Garlic
Peppercorns
Rosemary
Thyme

Flavour balancing (without adding fat)
Flavour enhancer
Reduces need for salt

Balsamic

Traditionally used for culinary purposes.

Specifically it is used for:-

Cooked meats
Desserts
Digestives
Gravies & Sauces
Salad seasoning
Tuna carpaccio
Vegetable flavouring

Rice

Rice vinegar is most popular in the cuisines of East and Southeast Asia.

Specifically it is used for:

Aromatic oriental dishes
Chicken
Fish
Pickling
Soups

Cane

Cane vinegar is made from sugar cane juice.

Specifically it is used for:

Herring, flavouring
Mustards
Pickling
Sauces
Sweet and sour dishes
Vinaigrettes

East Asian black, rice

Chinese black vinegar is made predominantly from rice.

Specifically it is used for:

Dipping sauce
Hot and sour sauce
Noodles
Salad dressings
Seafood dishes
Shark's fin soup
Soup
Sushi
Vegetable dressings

INDEX

SPOONS TO MILLILITRES

1/2 Teaspoon	2.5ml	1 Tablespoon	15ml
1 Teaspoon	5ml	2 Tablespoons	30ml
1-1/2 Teaspoons	7.5ml	3 Tablespoon	45ml
2 Teaspoons	10 ml	4 Tablespoons	60ml

GRAMS TO OUNCES

10g	0.25oz	225g	8oz
15g	0.38oz	250g	9oz
25g	1oz	275g	10oz
50g	2oz	300g	11oz
75g	3oz	350g	12oz
110g	4oz	375g	13oz
150g	5oz	400g	14oz
175g	6oz	425g	15oz
200g	7oz	450g	16oz

METRIC TO CUPS

Description	Metric	Cup
Flour etc	115g	1 cup
Clear Honey etc	350g	1 cup
Liquids	225ml	1 cup

LIQUID MEASURES

Fl oz	Pints	ml
5fl oz	1/4 pint	150ml
7.5fl oz		215ml
10fl oz	1/2 pint	275ml
15fl oz		425ml
20fl oz	1 pint	570ml
35fl oz	1-3/4 pints	1 litre

TEMPERATURE

Celsius	Fahrenheit	Gas Mark	Description
110c	225F	1/4	very cool
130c	250F	1/2	very cool
140c	275F	1	cool
150c	300F	2	cool
170c	325F	3	very moderate
180c	350F	4	moderate
190c	375F	5	moderate
200c	400F	6	moderately hot
220c	425F	7	hot
230c	450F	8	hot
240c	475F	9	very hot